D1547002

THE
UNIVERSITY OF WINNIPEG
PORTAGE & BALMORAL
WINNIPEG 2. MAN. CANADA
DISCARDED

POETRY & LIFE

# WALT WHITMAN & HIS POETRY

AMS PRESS
NEW YORK

Walt Whitman

# WALT WHITMAN & HIS POETRY

BY

HENRY BRYAN BINNS
Author of "A Life of Walt Whitman" "Abraham Lincoln" "The Great Companions" etc.

LONDON: GEORGE G.
HARRAP & COMPANY
2 & 3 PORTSMOUTH STREET
KINGSWAY W.C. MCMXV

One volume of the Poetry and Life Series
published by AMS Press

Reprinted by special arrangement with
George G. Harrap & Co. Ltd., London

From the edition of 1915, London

First AMS edition published in 1971

Manufactured in the United States of America

International Standard Book Number:
Complete Set: 0-404-52500-8
This Volume: 0-404-52502-4

Library of Congress Catalog Card Number: 75-120971

AMS PRESS INC.
NEW YORK, N.Y. 10003

# GENERAL PREFACE

A GLANCE through the pages of this little book will suffice to disclose the general plan of the series of which it forms a part. Only a few words of explanation, therefore, will be necessary.

The point of departure is the undeniable fact that with the vast majority of young students of literature a living interest in the work of any poet can best be aroused, and an intelligent appreciation of it secured, when it is immediately associated with the character and career of the poet himself. The cases are indeed few and far between in which much fresh light will not be thrown upon a poem by some knowledge of the personality of the writer, while it will often be found that the most direct—perhaps even the only—way to the heart of its meaning lies through a consideration of the circumstances in which it had its birth. The purely æsthetic critic may possibly object that a poem should be regarded simply as a self-contained and detached piece of art, having no personal affiliations or bearings. Of the validity of this as an abstract principle nothing need now be said. The fact remains that, in the earlier stages of study at any rate, poetry is most valued and loved when it is made to seem most human and vital; and the human and vital interest of poetry can be most surely brought home to the reader by the biographical method of interpretation.

This is to some exent recognized by writers of histories and text-books of literature, and by editors of selections from the works of our poets ; for place is always given by them to a certain amount of biographical material. But in the histories and text-books the biography of a given writer stands by itself, and his work has to be sought elsewhere, the student being left to make the connexion for himself ; while even in our current editions of selections there is little systematic attempt to link biography, step by step, with production.

This brings us at once to the chief purpose of the present series. In this, biography and production will be considered together and in intimate association. In other words, an endeavour will be made to interest the reader in the lives and personalities of the poets dealt with, and at the same time to use biography as an introduction and key to their writings.

Each volume will therefore contain the life-story of the poet who forms its subject. In this, attention will be specially directed to his personality as it expressed itself in his poetry, and to the influences and conditions which counted most as formative factors in the growth of his genius. This biographical study will be used as a setting for a selection, as large as space will permit, of his representative poems. Such poems, where possible, will be reproduced in full, and care will be taken to bring out their connexion with his character, his circumstances, and the movement of his mind. Then, in addition, so much more general literary criticism will be incorporated as may seem to be needed to supplement the biographical material, and to exhibit both the essential qualities and the historical importance of his work.

It is believed that the plan thus pursued is substantially in the nature of a new departure, and that the volumes of this series, constituting as they will an introduction to the study of some of our greatest poets, will be found useful to teachers and students of literature, and no less to the general lover of English poetry.

WILLIAM HENRY HUDSON

# POEMS QUOTED IN WHOLE

# POEMS QUOTED IN PART

# WALT WHITMAN AND HIS POETRY

MARKED personality is both attractive and repellent. Men born to some special work, above all men of the prophet type, divide the world into their partisans and opponents. For in such men strength and weakness are strangely blended. Is it that their defects actually belong to their qualities, that their failings are essential to their functions ? If they are to achieve their task, must they necessarily remain blind to their own limitations ? However we may answer these questions, our immediate affair is obviously with our own attitude toward such men. To remain indifferent to them is to lose something of the highest value, and something, besides, which men of the faultless temperament can never give. But to be blind to their failings, as their followers are, is to strain and mutilate our judgment. How are we to have ears for their words and yet discriminate between what is vital in them and what is not, what, moreover, is permanent and what merely occasional ?

Walt Whitman is manifestly of this type, and raises these questions. In the following pages, which attempt to give an introduction only, a first not a final view, I have written of him rather as of a personal friend than as a literary personage. I recognize his faults and his virtues ; I try to estimate his failure and success ; but for me these things are secondary to the man himself, whose personality outweighs them. Here, at the outset, I want to suggest the right relationship as between the reader and him. Whitman's work cannot yield its finer aroma to those who regard with indifference the man himself, as revealed in his poems. Its significance is reserved for his friends. And friends, surely, are those who are mutually pledged to candour ; between whom no blindness of prejudice or passion can subsist. To read Whitman aright one must have this clear-eyed affection.

Under the rudeness of his health lurks more that is shy and personal than you might suspect : he was lonely, and longed to give confidences. But, again, he may sometimes impose upon you. His very openness keeps back secrets. His cosmic catholicity conceals some of the limitations of a man driven by the necessity of his nature to protest. His original and profound view of life, of art, of America, set him in opposition to men who also had their vision. And though he always sought to see life whole, and to find his true relation to others in that whole, it must be confessed he did not always succeed. Moreover, he had the bias inseparable from a strongly marked personality. Thus we must not infrequently read back our poet into the fellowship of all the ages wherein he belongs, and from which he will sometimes run out.

We feel sometimes that he need not always have thought himself so solitary. Yet no one stands so much alone as the man of larger and more catholic spirit.

One cannot discuss Whitman and his poetry without raising a crop of difficult questions. These, of course, I cannot attempt to settle. As to poetry, all I need say here is simply that it is a form of expression, and must be adequately expressive. I am now, however, principally concerned about the thing expressed. Nowadays few readers will care to admit that they can get absolutely nothing out of "Leaves of Grass," but many will candidly confess they do not quite know what it is all about. Once the main theme is grasped the book becomes more or less comprehensible. Its lack of comprehensibility is never due so much to inadequacy of expression—or, in other words, to bad art—as to the perplexing character of the thing to be expressed. The theme, quite briefly put, is Whitman himself. Here is his own word for it :

"Leaves of Grass" . . . (I cannot too often reiterate) has mainly been the outcropping of my own emotional and other personal nature—an attempt, from first to last, to put *a Person*, a human being (myself, in the latter half of the nineteenth century, in America), freely, fully and truly on record. I could not find any similar personal record in current literature that satisfied me. But it is not on "Leaves of Grass" distinctively as *literature*, or a specimen thereof, that I feel to dwell, or advance claims. No one will get at my verses who insists upon viewing them as a literary

**performance, or attempt at such performance, or as aiming mainly toward art or æstheticism.**

Whitman wrote this as a postscript to his poems in 1888. Above all things he wanted to leave it clear that they were not so much a book as a man. He wanted his reader to recognize him behind the paper and ink, behind the words and ideas. He wanted to speak out of his pages, as one man to another, and to tell about himself.

The question remains, Was he really worth listening to? Was he indeed a notable and inspiring man, or merely, as many supposed, an egotistical old poseur? The best means of settling the question is unhappily no longer available: we cannot now turn in to the little house, 328 Mickle Street, Camden, and sit awhile, as so many others have done, with the old man himself. We must take their assurance of his significance. The big, simple, peasant-like old fellow, crippled by paralysis but still rosy-faced as a child, was so much and so profoundly alive that merely to sit near him was to become aware of a vitality rare among strong men. And something in his presence suggested that he kept company with august beings in that drab suburb of Philadelphia.

Of course, everybody did not find him attractive; and even to his friends he rarely revealed in conversation his inner life.

Many a true friend he had: the mere list of them is enough to make the heart glow with generous images; and he gave them of his best. But perhaps his only real confidants throughout his long life were the born readers of his "Leaves." To such, if they visited him, something in his companionship rather than in his talk corroborated and justified his poems, and was perhaps reassuring. Such reassurance must often have been welcome. For it is not every page that shines, as do so many, with its own clear and complete vindication.

In the Mickle Street days, it is true, Whitman was no longer the poet of 1855. No man can live a long life intensely and remain unchanged. But his personality was still tonic. We may call him an original, or a primitive, if these terms convey the notion of a character genuinely spontaneous, and as unconventional as though belonging to some different age or race. In some degree, at least, he had always borne this distinguishing quality; half a century earlier country boys had remarked it in their companion and teacher, just as Emerson and Howells felt it in the full vigour of his maturity. Thoreau's keen instinct uneasily sensed something more. "He is democracy," he commented after their interview. The phrase suggests that Whitman's seemingly simple nature was in reality a focus for many different and even divergent rays. He incorporated and coordinated in himself elements which in other men remain apart, contradictory and irreconcilable to one another. And though even Whitman was slow in recognizing his real self, and, as I shall point out, often failed to discriminate clearly between the sources of his poems, yet in these later days he gave the impression of harmony of soul, of wholeness and calm.

Such, at a first glimpse, was the personality Whitman sought to embody in his poems. True to the old identification of poet and creator, something virile and creative in him shed forth currents of personal influence, which, by the magic of his genius, still flow from his pages, putting his readers into contact not merely with his ideas and feelings, but with that ever-living, stimulating, inspiring person.

It may be that self-expression, that great mystery, is something more even than a necessity of the individual. It may answer to a common need, and be sanctioned by some requirement of the common life. And this may give to it not only its magical power, but its overwhelming urgency. Whitman tells us that when he put himself on record he did so not only in fulfilment of his own imperious conviction, but impelled by the commands of his whole nature, as irresistible as those that make the ocean flow or the globe revolve. Something in the deeps of him seemed to know its own significance for America, for Freedom, for Man. Out it must. He had no choice, as they say, but to give it utterance.

Not, be it understood, in the merely egotistical desire to "celebrate himself." Behind that famous phrase of his lies all his passionate devotion to the common average humanity out of which every person is wrought. What he assumes of himself, he requires you in your turn to assume. He challenges you to retort, in terms of your own manhood or womanhood more honourable yet. He regarded this as the only befitting modern attitude ; and supposed that America, the new world, could only be sung in chants resounding with the glory of ordinary humanity—its yet unexplored scope, its vista, its immortal reach and destiny. The supremacy over every circumstance of that divine Spirit who is Man, his incredible potentialities and eligibilities—these are Whitman's high themes, as they were, to the end, the subjects of his wonder and amaze. Of resolute purpose, he expressed these in terms of his own land and day. Thus, celebrating himself, a representative person, he was in the same sense celebrating nineteenth-century America, the America of Lincoln and Grant. And let us note that he, like Lincoln, belonged inalienably, by temperament and choice, to the 'common people,' whom in many respects he represented more fully than could the New England writers. For he sprang of a richer soil. Geographically these three great representatives of the war period came from the middle States—Lincoln, who was ten years Whitman's senior, out of Kentucky ; Grant, his junior, from Ohio ; and Whitman himself from the metropolitan State of New York.

But if Whitman's America was, in a sense, that of Grant and Lincoln, it was also his own. Like Mazzini's Italy, it was something more than an existent nation. Whitman's America stands in about the same relation to the America of the politicians as does Mazzini's Italy to that of the Triple Alliance. His new world is, indeed, a new world still, awaiting pioneers. For like the Polish Messianists he saw his country with the world-vision of the seer.

## I

WALT WHITMAN'S long life—he lived to be nearly seventy-three—was primarily devoted to deliberate, many-sided self-expression, and, *inter alia*, to the production of one book of chants or poems. This grew through a series of editions from a slender volume to one of 450 pages. Its first appearance in 1855, in his thirty-seventh year, divides his life into exactly equal periods, of preparation and achievement. He was born May 31, 1819, at West Hills, near Huntington, Long Island, and died at Camden, New Jersey, March 25, 1892. Other significant dates to be noted at once are the family's settlement in Brooklyn, in his fourth year ; his western and southern wanderings in his twenty-ninth ; his removal in his forty-third year from Brooklyn to Washington, where he worked among the wounded in the hospitals, continuing as a Government clerk till his first paralytic seizure in his fifty-fourth year, when he removed to Camden ; and his establishment in a cottage of his own in his sixty-fifth.

# WHITMAN & HIS POETRY

As to its men, the Whitman ancestry was sturdy but undistinguished. They had the excellent habit of marrying superior wives. Artisan and farming folk of English stock, Whitmans had lived in Long Island for more than a century before Walt was born. The original settlement of New York and a part of this district was Dutch, and a strong Dutch element remained. Cornelius van Velsor, Whitman's maternal grandfather—a jolly, round-voiced major who probably served in the recent war with England—had married into the large Welsh clan of Long Island Williamses. His wife's people were seamen and Quakers. His daughter, Whitman's mother, was a capable and very attractive, happy-natured woman. Well for her that she was, for Walter her husband, the carpenter and house-builder, was an independent, strong-headed man, of a difficult, unsuccessful type ; and her large family afforded cause enough for anxiety. Jesse, the eldest of nine, remained a labourer and ended his days in an asylum. Another was not much more fortunate ; the fifth died in infancy ; while the youngest was an imbecile. On the other side of the account, two of the sons successfully established themselves, one rising to a colonelcy in the Civil War, the other becoming an engineer ; one of the daughters at least seems to have taken after her mother ; and besides—showing, I think, a clear profit on the family balance-sheet—there remains the subject of this study.

Grandfather Jesse, under whose roof the little 'Walt' was born and spent his earliest years, counted as a personal friend that singular local worthy, the Quaker preacher Elias Hicks. Grandmother Whitman was a woman of some education and 'solid character.' Their shingled farmhouse—then new—lies, with its well, its outbuildings and orchard, under the wooded crown of those Huntington Hills that form the backbone of the 'fish-shaped island'—Paumànok of the Indians. Though it is not many miles from Brooklyn, it is still in a remote countryside; its lanes bordered with huckleberry and golden-rod, its woods full of birds. From the hill-ridge you can see the coast-line of Connecticut, northward, across the narrow Sound. Southward, too, on a clear day, your eye will sweep over the sloping meadow-lands to another and farther stretch of sea. In Whitman's boyhood it was, of course, even more purely rural, a Bœotia adjacent to the metropolis. Its social life was that of a vigorous agricultural and fishing community, with democratic customs and friendly hospitality.

Though his father removed to Brooklyn, house-building, when Walt was quite a youngster, the lad spent a large part of his time in Long Island, either at the old farm or elsewhere, during all the first half of his life. He shared the Long Islander's passion for the sea, loved especially its fisher-folk and pilots and the movement and music of the shore; was first filled with the desire for expression by the sight of a ship under full sail; but also he loved the woods and the wide landscape peopled by those "powerful uneducated persons" to whose intercourse he owed the better half of his irregular education.

A century ago even New York was by no means the bloated, nerve-shattering maelstrom of to-day; Brooklyn was but a country town, the East River still unbridged. The Whitmans lived at first on the water-side close to Fulton Ferry. Walt went to school, and to Sunday school; pored over the "Arabian Nights," and, later, Sir Walter Scott; became an office-boy; at thirteen was put to printing; began to live away from home, to scribble verses and to gloat over their appearance in the "Long Island Patriot." Now, too, crossing the Ferry on every possible occasion, he began to explore the city on Manhattan Island opposite. He loved its full, vivid life, the rush of Broadway, the varied excitement of its great political meetings, lectures, sermons; above all, the wonder-land of its theatres, to which his Press ticket freely admitted him. It was an enormously stimulating life for an intelligent, receptive lad. Too stimulating for an emotional one. It is with a breath of relief that one finds him, at seventeen, back in the country, where for the next four years he very profitably taught school, studied, had famous holidays all along the coast, and experimented on his own account in local journalism. I always like to think of that boyish enterprise, his founding of the "Long Islander" just as he turned nineteen. Buying press and type, he set up his paper in a loft looking out on the main street of Huntington; then he purchased a serviceable horse, and went of an evening far afield with his wares along the glimmering roads, through the dark woodland strips and across that broad, friendly country, where every house was open to him. He was still a boy, perhaps, as some say, a phenomenally lazy boy, and presently the first enthusiasm flagged. One cannot wonder. He had shot up to his full six feet two by the time he was fifteen, and those next years were the season for inner growth, not for establishing newspapers. He was 'taking in' all the time; observing, enjoying, experiencing; putting out his strength first in one direction, then in another. A delightful companion when he was in the companionable mood, but that was not always. He had a way and will of his own; something, too, of his father's difficult quality, which brought him often into conflict with that silent, passionate man.

In 1841, at twenty-two, he entered the New York office of the "New World." Verses and short stories over his name or initials now began to appear in the principal metropolitan magazines, notably in the "Democratic Review," which at this time numbered among its contributors such mature writers as Whittier, Bryant, Hawthorne and Longfellow. As a sample of this early work I will quote the concluding verses of "Each has his Grief," contributed to the "New World" in November 1841.

So welcome death! Whene'er the time
  That the dread summons must be met,
I'll yield without one pang of fear,
  Or sigh, or vain regret.

But like unto a weary child,
  That, over field and wood all day
Has ranged and struggled, and at last,
  Worn out with toil and play,

Goes up at evening to his home,
  And throws him, sleepy, tired and sore,
Upon his bed and rests him there,
  His pain and trouble o'er.

On the same page of the magazine appears an "Original Tale. The Child's Champion. By Walter Whitman." It was afterwards reprinted by him, with alterations, in his "Complete Prose" as "The Boy and the Profligate."

His temperance tale of "Franklin Evans" was issued as a supplement to the same magazine a year later. Though at the moment it won a gratifying success, it has all the faults of an immature author's experiment in a medium wholly foreign to his real bent. After many vicissitudes and short sojourns as editor, now in one office, now in another, he took charge, in February 1846, of the "Brooklyn Daily Eagle," a local Democratic sheet with an office by the Ferry. For two years he conducted it with vigour and an independence that eventually brought him into conflict with the owners. For if, like Bryant, he belonged to the Democratic party, he was a member of its left wing. He came of ardent Anti-slavery stock, and now proclaimed himself a 'Free-soiler' when the policy of refusing to extend slave-territory was dividing his party. The schism in New York State was especially critical, and let in the last Whig President. Whitman can hardly have regretted that. He hated the jingo policy of the outgoing Democrat, Polk. In the "Eagle" he had described war as "the greatest curse that can befall a people, and the bitterest obstacle to the progress of all those high and true reforms that make the glory of this age above the darkness of the ages past and gone." This rather awkward sentence is very characteristic of the young Whitman, always an ardent reformer. And therewith a keen politician, interesting himself especially in local matters, as, for example, the securing of a public park for Brooklyn ; but yet never forgetting the national issue. Since it was his outspoken Anti-slavery attitude that drove him from the "Eagle," it is interesting that his next engagement should have taken him to the slave-capital itself, to help found the "Crescent," not, we may suppose, in the slave-owners' interest.

# WHITMAN & HIS POETRY

## II

EIGHTEEN hundred and forty-eight, the year of revolutions, celebrated in one of the earliest of Whitman's characteristic chants, marks also the commencement of a new phase in his personal liberation. He had declared his independence by sacrificing his post on a matter of fundamental principle; now he was to look abroad into a wider world, to wander in leisurely fashion through thousands of miles of new and varied lands—yet all American—and amid that romantic wandering to be initiated, as I think, into the mysteries of passion.

He was twenty-nine. The articles and verses of his early manhood indicate no preoccupation with romance. Yet Whitman's was an intensely emotional, impressionable nature. No one who reads the "Song of Myself" can question this, or doubt its writer's preoccupation with sex at the period of its inception. There are hints scattered over his writings, notably in "Out of the Cradle," that, healthy and happy as he was, he yet suffered in early life from the passionate stress and growing pains of an imaginative temperament. His early verses and stories turn upon death and tragic incidents, suggesting that he was long at grips with stubborn questionings. For all his optimism, his sunny nature, his exulting faith, he showed even in later years moods of sombre hue. Gay-hearted, "amazed at his own lightness and glee," he was yet by no means unacquainted with the dreadful and the sinister. Moreover, he was comparatively late in finding self-expression, and long seeking it. The real Whitman, yet undiscovered, must have been a difficult, rebellious companion to the young ambitious journalist and politician.

But, whatever his difficulties, his nature was fundamentally sweet and sane and clean. He had even a half-Puritan quality: he served each reformist cause of the hour with ardour. He had his dandiacal phase, high hat, frock-coat, and jaunty button-hole. It seems to me that his very sensitiveness to emotion, his marked delicacy of sight and touch and hearing, his immense capacity for response and sympathy, demanded a firm groundwork of reserve and deliberate self-control, if he were to keep that health and self-possession upon which he especially prided himself even as a lad. Dissipation did not attract him. But life did. Almost terrifyingly, life drew him, more and more. Each year his faith in life grew able to accept more. Naturally individual and self-willed, he became increasingly unconventional, and, for a time, definitely 'Bohemian' in his way of living. But 'Bohemian' after an American rather than a European pattern. Doubtless his Southern journey, bringing him into contact with the French life of old New Orleans, broke through old habits and left his mind surging with new experience. Precisely what the whole episode signified to him personally we shall probably never know. He evidently did not intend us to. But for him the South was ever after associated with passionate desire. Whitman never married. We need not think of him as "the Great God Pan"; but it is not easy to imagine him domesticated. If he ever truly mated it must have been with some nature as free and unconventional as his own. Such a woman he may have found in New Orleans, perhaps, as M. Bazalgette suggests, a French 'Bohemian'; as passionate, and even less conventional than he was. Much might be explained if we could so read the story. It may have been she that justified to him things hitherto outcast and alien. If she became the mother of his children—grandmother of that Southern lad who came to visit him shortly before his death—his relation with her must have been for him at once tragic and profoundly liberating.

His verses "Sailing the Mississippi at Midnight" breathe a certain dread of unknown passional experiences ready to take him at unawares and overwhelm him:

> . . . When there comes a voluptuous languor,
> Soft the sunshine, silent the air,
> Bewitching your craft with safety and sweetness,
> Then, young pilot of life, beware!

But the great outburst of his succeeding years is that of a spirit freed from any haunting distrust of life and its mysteries. He has now made the personal discovery that sanely passionate living is in nowise hostile to the needs of the inner life. In the "Song of Myself" his faith in life is whole-hearted, he has no vestige of fear left. He has known life at full-tide and given himself to living. He is sorry for those to whom it can seem cruel or treacherous. It has not shown itself such to him. For him "all has been gentle." For him "creation is the friend whose embracing awakes" him.

The insistence on this evangel suggests the passing of some dreadful doubt. His manhood has met with unhoped-for assurance of its own sanity and glory. I think the discovery intoxicated him for a time. During the ensuing years in New York "he sounded all experiences of life, with all their passions, pleasures, and abandonments." He admitted in later years that at this period his life was not above criticism. But he neither explained nor apologized. Obviously he was not a pattern for imitators to reproduce. With all his faults, which it would serve no good purpose to minimize, and which he himself acknowledged, he remains a challenge; and on the whole a wholesome shock to preconceived ideas. No one can read the full-throated love-poem "Out of the Cradle," with its haunting theme of passion and parting, and maintain that Whitman was merely a robustious human animal.

It must have been about 1849, after the fall of Mazzini's Roman Republic, that he wrote those lines on the failure of the popular risings in Europe which end with the quatrain,

> Not a disembodied spirit
> Can the weapons of tyrants let loose,
> But it shall stalk invisibly over the earth,
> Whispering, counselling, cautioning.

These, quoted in a lecture to the Brooklyn Art Union in 1851, he afterwards incorporated in "Leaves of Grass." Other early poems in free-rhythm were contributed during the next few years either to Bryant's "Evening Post" or Horace Greeley's "Tribune." Of these, "Wounded in the House of Friends" may, like Whittier's "Ichabod," have been occasioned by Webster's support of Clay's Compromise in 1850. "Blood-money" belongs either to the same period or to 1854, a year in which he must have written his "Boston Ballad" on the arrest of a fugitive slave in that city. The Scriptural, prophetic quality of these early outpourings is obvious in such lines as those with which "Blood-money" opens :

> Of olden time when it came to pass
> That the beautiful god, Jesus, should finish his
>     work on earth,
> Then went Judas and sold the divine youth,
> And took pay for the body . . .
> . . . And still Iscariot plies his trade.

For all his father's admiration of Tom Paine, Whitman had been well grounded in Bible knowledge. And the volume was always companionable to him. His earliest and longest-lived ambition was to contribute a new American book to the collected holy writ of all the ages. Faith, according to the best Quaker doctrine such as Hicks had preached, lays hold anew in each age upon actual inspiration, seizing the Divine purpose, hearing and uttering forth anew the creative word.

Paine's name recalls an equally adventurous Republican spirit who deeply influenced Whitman's youth. In 1852 died Fanny Wright, the brilliant and generous woman to whose addresses in old Tammany Hall he had listened spellbound as a boy. She was another of the objects of his father's fervent admiration. In his last years Whitman spoke of her with all the enthusiasm due to his boyhood's first love. She was thirty-six when he was twelve. I do not doubt that it was she who stamped upon his soul that image of free and independent womanhood which is never absent from his pages. Her death would quicken again the old days when, in his own emphatic words, "she possessed herself of my body and soul."

On his return to Brooklyn Whitman had first opened a small printing office and bookshop beside his favourite Ferry, and for two years had published the "Freeman." Then he felt the need of other occupation, and joined his father, now over sixty, in building and selling frame-houses in the rapidly growing town. He lived on at home in the independent, free fashion of a self-sufficient man of thirty, accustomed to being loved and to having his own way. He was made much of by his mother, and by other women; and in all directions he was humoured and respected: partly for his natural solidity and judgment; partly, perhaps, because there was a "fire eligible to leap forth" from beneath the kindly good-nature.

These leisurely years spent in and about New York among his own folk were all-important for the form and content of the work he was now preparing. If his Southern journey had shown him America as he had never before been able to realize her, in all her blended promise and peril—the mighty river, the Mississippi; Missouri and the great new West, where the 'Free-soil' struggle was to be so bitterly waged; the French South, where slavery had its capital; the return by way of Chicago, and Niagara with Canada in view—yet it was the ever more tremendous flow of human life through the metropolis, its tumultuous movement and infinitely varied expression, that filled his mind with thronging pictures and vast rhythms. It was New York, flooded afresh with a torrent of exiles from reactionary Europe, New York the gateway to a new world of promise, the last refuge of liberty on the earth, it was New York that held him in those years when other men were striking west for California or Kansas.

Beside great exiles like Kossuth, came the actors and singers of the world; best of all for Whitman came Alboni, whose perfect voice, with its rare impersonal fascination, seemed to open to him some new door of self-expression. Then, too, in that age of tremendous material development—all of it intensely exciting to Whitman—that age of applied discoveries, railways, steamships, telegraphs—invention displayed its miracles before his greedy eyes in the galleries of the World's Fair; where also European painting and sculpture had some scanty representation. The beautiful, busy Bay was full of those swift clipper-ships he delighted to watch; while over the Ferry and through the streets of the city moved continually—for all the existent corruption, the political and social *laissez-faire*—the figures of a vivid democratic life. Whitman spent hours together on the Broadway coaches, abandoned to the sheer enjoyment of the scene. Sometimes he took the reins, as when one winter one of his driver friends lay in hospital with a family unprovided for; sometimes he took the wheel on the ferry-boat; but for the main part he was simply satisfied to absorb that amazing life and movement. Its ever-varying flow and rhythm of flowing exhilarated him—movement of crowds on the pavements, movement of surf on the beach, movement of rivers, movement of sailing-ships, movement of clouds and birds across the sky. He loved to associate with the men who participated in all this, seamen and pilots, ferry-men and stage-drivers. From that association he seemed to catch, in its human expression, something of the flow and cadence of these major rhythms. Withal, as I have said, he did not forget the minor. He was no stranger to the dark places of the city. He was familiar with the outcast and the unfortunate, women and men.

Probably it was on a "transparent summer morning" in 1853, in one of his many vacations from manual labour, that, away in the meadows of Long Island, Whitman had the mystical experience recorded, or rather suggested, in the fifth section of the "Song of Myself." Whatever it was, it brought him permanent conviction of the infinite significance of every object to the awakened soul, absolute intuitive certainty of God, of immortality, of a purposive plan running through creation and of his own part in it. Whether or no it was the first of such moments of illumination we are not told. Others occurred afterwards throughout his life. There were besides many curious psychic visions and journeyings suggested in otherwise obscure passages of his poems. All such hints of a mystical experience shared by comparatively few of his readers lend themselves to misunderstanding. It is one of the greatest difficulties besetting Whitman's poems that they so often deal with the high latitudes of human life as yet unfamiliar and inadequately explored. His consciousness extended into ranges beyond those commonly accessible. Hence he is suspect by the narrower type of intelligence. His abnormality, which, since he kept the due balance of his mind and did not allow any one element of his experience to overweigh it, was actually a superiority of consciousness—this abnormality is often cited against him. But it was an integral part of his genius, intimately bound up with his capacity for inspiration. All genius, all inspiration—save that which has been more or less sterilized by processes of explanation during centuries—is indeed suspect, and would, I suppose, be eliminated by 'eugenic' processes in the name of the established order of things, if this narrower intelligence had its way; for the reason that genius rejects its laws and standards as hostile to the real purpose and freedom of a full-grown manhood.

While there can be no question of Whitman's wide psychic experience, however we may describe it, it seems to have had no obvious relation with the curious outbreak of spiritualistic phenomena then rife in America. I do not know that he took special interest in the "Rochester knockings," or the revelations and materializations of mediums; though of course he must have shared the widespread interest in the problems they raised. His experiences were of a different type, and, as I think, upon a different level. Moreover, in a sense, they were actually opposed to those others, for whereas there is a general tendency for the latter to disintegrate the personality, to weaken its central citadel of will and conscious purpose, Whitman's reinforced and strengthened his. And they did so because, to use his own word, he never 'abased' himself to them: because, while he refused to doubt or reject, he also refused to allow this side of his nature, this "electric self," to usurp upon his ordinary faculties or to subject his will. In later life he wrote "about the shows of life" and his experience in them: "I am deeper and deeper impressed, the older I grow, that *the real something has yet to be known.* It is well I am physically ballasted so strong, with weightiest animality and appetites, or I should go off in a balloon." The intense reality of these experiences, which obviously can only be hinted at here, is suggested in many passages of "Leaves of Grass," and in this rejected couplet:

I cannot be awake, for nothing looks to me as it did before;
Or else I am awake for the first time, and all before has been a mean sleep.

He himself associated them with his perfect physical health, raised as it were to a spiritual, or let us say a visionary power. In one of the latest paragraphs of his "Complete Prose"[1] he wrote:

In that condition the whole body is elevated to a state by others unknown—inwardly and outwardly illuminated, purified, made solid, strong, yet buoyant. A singular charm, more than beauty, flickers out of, and over, the face—a curious transparency beams in the eyes, both in the iris and the white—the temper partakes also. Nothing that happens—no event, rencontre, weather, etc.—but it is confronted—nothing but is subdued into sustenance—such is the

[1] Page 502.

marvellous transformation from the old timorousness and the old process of causes and effects. Sorrows and disappointments cease—there is no more borrowing trouble in advance. A man realizes the venerable myth—he is a god walking the earth, he sees new eligibilities, powers and beauties everywhere ; he himself has a new eyesight and hearing.

## III

AFTER some three or four years, the house-building was finally abandoned, a few months before old Walter Whitman's death. By that time his son was fully occupied in the last redaction of his "Leaves of Grass," which appeared a few days before his father's decease. Walt—as he chose to be called, and as he signed himself from this time forward—had been working upon it for several years : putting it by to take it out again when the urgent need arose, writing and re-writing it. The first serious resolve to put himself on record must have been made in his thirtieth year.

He wrote his poems largely out of doors, jotting down their ideas fragmentarily on scraps of paper or little rough note-books made of sheets folded together. These he brooded over constantly, gradually finding a continuity in the fragments, and building them into a whole. Often he would pause to write in the midst of his work, or take out his pencil at the opera, or on a stage-top in mid Broadway, wherever, in fact, the inspiration seized him. When alone he declaimed his lines aloud, trying them over and testing their reality against that of the living concrete world ; patiently and resolutely eliminating whatever stood condemned by that test, whatever smelt of the lamp or savoured of the indoor-conventional. It was to be a book for outdoor America ; to give this new people consciousness of its identity, its personality, its own spiritual needs and promise as distinct from all other. Never was book less bookish.

The form that he found, though primarily corresponding to certain rhythms and sequences of movement in nature, owes something to Carlyle and Emerson's prose, something to the cadences of Italian opera, much to oratory, more to the rhythms of the Jacobean Bible. Ossian was a warning rather than an example to him ; so, surely, was Martin Tupper. He probably did not know Blake's prophetic books ; but he must certainly have seen that singular mystical rhapsody on the English Crystal Palace of 1850, Warren's "The Lily and the Bee." As Mr. Perry has pointed out, this offered him a complete scaffolding for his own edifice. I need hardly say that Whitman was no mere plagiarist. His genius was creative, and the creator is rarely conscious of his debt to those who have forerun him. Emerson noted his kinship with the Orientals ; saying mischievously that his form was a cross between that of the "New York Herald" and the "Bhagavad-gita." Whitman does not seem to have read the current translations of the Eastern writings, but the kinship is none the less striking. His great favourites, Homer and the Greek tragedians, Dante's "Inferno," and the Bible itself, were the translated classics of other nations, necessarily divested of their original form. His choice among English poets was for the dramatic Shakespeare, the Scots balladists, the songs of Burns. These seem to indicate his preference for rhythms of declamation or song rather than more studied and elaborate metrical arrangements. Indeed, the form and cadence of Whitman's poems can often only be appreciated when they are given vocal rendering. Their music does not reveal itself to the eye alone. They were written to be declaimed. They are monologues, recitatives, arias, and anthems. They call out for the voice, and for a responding audience. Some demand a singer accompanied by full orchestra, some may ask for choral treatment. They spring out of the heart of a time when oratory was the breath of political life, and when political life absorbed the best thought of America.

That a compelling sense of form, and the study of its principles, was by no means lacking in Whitman is evident in the pages of his 1855 preface, wherein he defines the new poetry as corresponding to the life of America :

> The Americans, of all nations at any time upon the earth, have probably the fullest poetical nature. The United States themselves are essentially the greatest poem. . . . Here at last is something in the doings

of man that corresponds with the broadcast doings of the day and night. . . . Here is action untied from strings, necessarily blind to particulars and details, magnificently moving in masses.

He proceeds to suggest his idea of poetic form;

The poetic quality is not marshal'd in rhyme or uniformity, or abstract addresses to things, nor in melancholy complaints or good precepts, but is the life of these and much else, and is in the soul. The profit of rhyme is that it drops seeds of a sweeter and more luxuriant rhyme, and of uniformity that it conveys itself into its own roots in the ground out of sight. The rhyme and uniformity of perfect poems show the free growth of metrical laws, and bud from them as unerringly and loosely as lilacs and roses on a bush, and take shapes as compact as the shapes of chestnuts and oranges, and melons and pears, and shed the perfume impalpable to form. The fluency and ornaments of the finest poems . . . are not independent but dependent. All beauty comes from beautiful blood and a beautiful brain. If the greatnesses are in conjunction in a man or woman, it is enough—the fact will prevail through the universe; but the gaggery and gilt of a million years will not prevail. Who troubles himself about his ornaments or fluency is lost. This is what you shall do: Love the earth and sun and the animals, despise riches, give alms to every one that asks, stand up for the stupid and crazy, devote your income and labour to others, hate tyrants, argue not concerning God, have patience and indulgence toward the people, take off your hat to nothing known or unknown, or to any man or number of men—go freely with powerful uneducated persons, and with the young, and with the mothers of families—[read these leaves in the open air every season of every year in your life [1]]—re-examine all you have been told in school or church or in any book, and dismiss whatever insults your own soul; and your very flesh shall be a great poem, and have the richest fluency, not only in its words, but in the silent lines of its lips and face, and between the lashes of your eyes, and in every motion and joint of your body. The poet shall not spend his time in unneeded work. He shall know that the ground is already plough'd and manured; others may not know it but he shall. He shall go directly to the creation.

He urges that

The art of art, the glory of expression and the sunshine of the light of letters, is simplicity. Nothing is better than simplicity—nothing can make up for excess, or for the lack of definiteness. . . . To speak in literature with the perfect rectitude and insouciance of the movements of animals, and the unimpeachableness of the sentiment of trees in the woods and grass by the roadside, is the flawless triumph of art. If you have look'd on him who has achiev'd it, you have look'd on one of the masters of the artists of all nations and times. You shall not contemplate the flight of the gray gull over the bay, or the mettlesome action of the blood horse, or the tall leaning of sunflowers on their stalk, or the appearance of the sun journeying through heaven, or the appearance of the moon afterward, with any more satisfaction than you shall contemplate him. The great poet has less a mark'd style and is more the channel of thoughts and things without increase or

[1] This clause in brackets only appears in the 1855 version; I quote the rest from the portions republished in "Complete Prose."

diminution, and is the free channel of himself. He swears to his art, I will not be meddlesome. . . . What I tell I tell for precisely what it is. . . . What I experience or portray shall go from my composition without a shred of my composition. You shall stand by my side and look in the mirror with me.

The writer of this preface already proves himself a master of words. To fulfil the large programme he had thus framed for the American poet was another matter, and Whitman realized that at the best he could do no more than strike a few preluding chords and make a beginning. All honour to him for setting so high the standard by which he himself must be measured. Let it be admitted that only at his greatest moments of undeniable inspiration does he succeed. The admission carries with it sufficient vindication. Both for his poems and his life, he is his own most implacable judge : he demands that none should essay to corrupt justice for him or his. But in his claim for this unmixed justice he also demands that the verdict of successful achievement should be refused those cunning makers of tinkling verse who have never even conceived what it means to be a poet.

Against these daring passages of challenge and promise may be set one of the notes in which Whitman has described the actual travail of self-expression : "The beating flights of wings, uncertain where you will soar or bring up—or whether you will soar at all—to end perhaps in ignominious fall and failure ! Those toils and struggles of baffled, impeded articulation

—those moods of proudest ambition and daring, quickly followed by deeper moods of qualm, despair, utter distrust of one's self—those years of venture and callow formation! —unfoldings so copious, often inopportune . . . a meagre dot or dash of genuine light at best."

This is not the place, nor have I space here at my disposal, to treat of the intimate relation between faith and poetic inspiration. The critical analytic faculty cannot, by its pedestrian nature, attain to those ethereal regions wherein the creative forces have their dwelling. Only the winged intelligence can ascend thither, and the soul cannot exercise its flying power without faith. True imagination is inseparable from faith. The freedom and virility of Whitman's faith are at the very root of his creative work. They gave him not only a new perspective, they filled his body and mind with the pulsating rhythm of a life larger than the merely individual. Faith, indeed, he shared with all aspiring souls. But each man's faith is coloured by his personality. If the soul's flight depends directly on its faith, then the character of Whitman's faith is well suggested by Rudolf Schmidt when he speaks of this poet's inspiration as akin to "the flight of the eagle."

When the oft-rewritten manuscript was finally complete, he took it to a little printing office in Brooklyn, and helped to set up its long, flowing lines, which never looked so much in place as on the ample pages of that dark green slender volume, now so rare. During this time Walt's irregular hours were a natural source of irritation to the household. Things became easier when, the book being finished, he took himself off to the far end of Long Island for the remainder of the summer, to consider his work at leisure before going forward with it. To reconsider and to rest. The completion of the slender book can have been no child's play. The forward swing and momentum which it carries and projects witness to the titanic character of its original œstrum. The current from his "electric self" was then at its highest voltage!

Whitman regarded his book as the poem of his personality, and the first and longest of his poems is definitely entitled "Song of Myself." It may not afford an all-round view of the man as others saw him, and it is obviously symbolical rather than realistic in its relation to its subject. But with its large, loose, masterly treatment, it is an extraordinarily interesting portrayal. And one remembers that its author explicitly declined to remove from later editions passages against which his friends and even his own maturer taste protested, because, without them, the portrait would lose certain essential attributes. He did, however, considerably modify this first version in later years. I quote from the final rendering.

> I celebrate myself, and sing myself,
> And what I assume you shall assume,
> For every atom belonging to me as good belongs
> to you.

I loafe and invite my soul,
I lean and loafe at my ease observing a spear of
summer grass.

My tongue, every atom of my blood, form'd from
this soil, this air,
Born here of parents born here from parents the
same, and their parents the same,
I, now thirty-seven years old in perfect health
begin,
Hoping to cease not till death.

Creeds and schools in abeyance,
Retiring back a while sufficed at what they are,
but never forgotten,
I harbour for good or bad, I permit to speak at every
hazard,
Nature without check with original energy.

Thus commencing, he proceeds to unfold his theme through that tumultuous succession of moods and movements—ejaculations, observations, interrogations—which forms the ever-changing body of his tremendous chant. Often it lacks humour ; sometimes that very note of mere self-assertion which he sought to exclude rings with its thin, false tone through the great music ; but, strangely unhindered, page after page, the lines swing forward, evoking for us the essential, elemental Walt Whitman, the "caresser of life" out of whom "the look of the bay mare" has "shamed silliness." Everything seems significant to him : he reads Nature like an open book ; her creatures converse with him, for he knows himself akin to each. Yet he knows also his own place, wherein he is lord. Withal, he wears his hat with a defiant, self-sufficient cock: he is "solid and sound," permanent, august as any.

My foothold is tenon'd and mortis'd in granite,
I laugh at what you call dissolution
And I know the amplitude of time.

He subscribes himself the companion of the sea and the earth's lover:

I am he that walks with the tender and growing night,
I call to the earth and sea half-held by the night.

Press close bare-bosom'd night—press close magnetic nourishing night!
Night of south winds—night of the large few stars!
Still nodding night—mad naked summer night.

Smile O voluptuous cool-breath'd earth!
Earth of the slumbering and liquid trees!
Earth of departed sunset—earth of the mountains misty-topt!
Earth of the vitreous pour of the full moon just tinged with blue!
Earth of shine and dark mottling the tide of the river!
Earth of the limpid gray of clouds brighter and clearer for my sake!
Far-swooping elbow'd earth—rich apple-blossom'd earth!
Smile, for your lover comes.

Prodigal, you have given me love—therefore I to you give love!
O unspeakable passionate love.

He accepts vice along with virtue ; but is amazed at a mean man or an infidel, for his own faith "never balks." He "goes on the square," but beats the "gong of revolt." Then follows this singular auto-description :

> Walt Whitman, a kosmos, of Manhattan the son,
> Turbulent, fleshy, sensual, eating, drinking and breeding,
> No sentimentalist, no stander above men and women or apart from them,
> No more modest than immodest.

And close on its heels :

> Whoever degrades another degrades me. . . .

Giving a voice to whatever was regarded as outcast and indecent, he—this cosmic, democratic fellow, this man who feels himself divine inside and out—will clarify and transfigure it out of shame. He is filled with that pantheistic wonder which is the nebula of aspiration, at all the miracle of life ; and this he balances and offsets with the dominant spiritual fact of creative personality—he challenges the very sunrise with equal spiritual glories. But he recognizes the incommunicable nature of that final word which is himself.

Many passages assert the keenness of his sympathetic emotion. He carries antennæ, as it were, "instant conductors all over me"—making him almost too ready a prey to emotional assault. A leaf of grass or a farmer's girl boiling her tea-kettle may arouse in him a passion of adoration and wonder. Is it this hypersensitiveness that makes him turn to the animals ?

I think I could turn and live with animals, they
are so placid and self-contain'd,
I stand and look at them long and long.

They do not sweat and whine about their condition,
They do not lie awake in the dark and weep for
their sins,
They do not make me sick discussing their duty
to God,
Not one is dissatisfied, not one is demented with
the mania of owning things,
Not one kneels to another, nor to his kind that
lived thousands of years ago,
Not one is respectable or unhappy over the whole
earth.

He affirms his psychic power to pass in vision to and fro through time and space, a disembodied traveller, possessing himself out of the past of immense ranges of human and subhuman experience, so that it becomes, in a sense, personal to him and his own. He feels and assimilates into his own life the agonies as well as the ecstasies of the world : he is not afraid to open his heart to them.

I understand the large hearts of heroes,
The courage of present times and all times,
How the skipper saw the crowded and rudderless
wreck of the steam-ship, and Death chasing
it up and down the storm,

How he knuckled tight and gave not back an inch, and was faithful of days and faithful of nights,
And chalk'd in large letters on a board, *Be of good cheer, we will not desert you* ;
How he follow'd with them and tack'd with them three days and would not give it up,
How he saved the drifting company at last,
How the lank loose-gown'd women look'd when boated from the side of their prepared graves,
How the silent old-faced infants and the lifted sick, and the sharp-lipp'd unshaved men ;
All this I swallow, it tastes good, I like it well, it becomes mine,
I am the man, I suffer'd, I was there.

The disdain and calmness of martyrs,
The mother of old, condemn'd for a witch, burnt with dry wood, her children gazing on,
The hounded slave that flags in the race, leans by the fence, blowing, cover'd with sweat,
The twinges that sting like needles his legs and neck, the murderous buckshot and the bullets,
All these I feel or am.

I am the hounded slave, I wince at the bite of the dogs,
Hell and despair are upon me, crack and again crack the marksmen,
I clutch the rails of the fence, my gore dribs, thinn'd with the ooze of my skin,
I fall on the weeds and stones,
The riders spur their unwilling horses, haul close,
Taunt my dizzy ears and beat me violently over the head with whip-stocks.

Agonies are one of my changes of garments,
I do not ask the wounded person how he feels, I
myself become the wounded person,
My hurts turn livid upon me as I lean on a cane
and observe.

Yet from all these experiences, all this vicarious suffering, he emerges with undiminished vitality, "replenished with supreme power." He is the "friendly and flowing savage" whose company everybody covets, for the sake of a personality that gives itself forth as lavishly as the sunshine or as the perfume of a flower; an inexhaustible spring of creative life, good not only to heal the sick but roughly and boisterously to shake the soul of man out of its preposterous attitude of self-depreciation. He was, or rather he is, a tremendous revulsion from that attitude: as such he expresses himself with exaggeration and violence, with eager colloquial self-assertion.

Behold, I do not give lectures or a little charity,
When I give I give myself.

You there, impotent, loose in the knees,
Open your scarf'd chops till I blow grit within you,
Spread your palms and lift the flaps of your pockets,
I am not to be denied, I compel, I have stores
plenty and to spare,
And anything I have I bestow. . . .

To any one dying, thither I speed and twist the
knob of the door,
Turn the bed-clothes toward the foot of the bed,
Let the physician and the priest go home.

I seize the descending man and raise him with
resistless will,
O despairer, here is my neck,
By God, you shall not go down ! hang your whole
weight upon me.

I dilate you with tremendous breath, I buoy you up,
Every room of the house do I fill with an arm'd
force,
Lovers of me, bafflers of graves.

Sleep—I and they keep guard all night,
Not doubt, not decease shall dare to lay finger
upon you,
I have embraced you, and henceforth possess you
to myself,
And when you rise in the morning you will find
what I tell you is so.

Regarding himself, as by his function the poet may, as a type and symbol of man, he stands at the crown of creation :

I am an acme of things accomplish'd, and I an
encloser of things to be.

My feet strike an apex of the apices of the stairs,
On every step bunches of ages, and larger bunches
between the steps,
All below duly travel'd, and still I mount and
mount.

Rise after rise bow the phantoms behind me,
Afar down I see the huge first Nothing, I know I
was even there,
I waited unseen and always, and slept through the
lethargic mist,

And took my time, and took no hurt from the
fetid carbon.

Long I was hugg'd close—long and long.

Immense have been the preparations for me,
Faithful and friendly the arms that have help'd
me.

Cycles ferried my cradle, rowing and rowing like
cheerful boatmen,
For room to me stars kept aside in their own
rings,
They sent influences to look after what was to
hold me.

Before I was born out of my mother generations
guided me,
My embryo has never been torpid, nothing could
overlay it.

For it the nebula cohered to an orb,
The long slow strata piled to rest it on,
Vast vegetables gave it sustenance,
Monstrous sauroids transported it in their mouths
and deposited it with care.

All forces have been steadily employ'd to complete
and delight me,
Now on this spot I stand with my robust soul.

He is sure, also, of his goal :

My rendezvous is appointed, it is certain,
The Lord will be there and wait till I come on
perfect terms.

He hates mere conformity and fear, and any virtue bred of such : vice itself seems less ugly to him than fear. A man should stand composed and undoubting in the face of the universe. For in spite of every appearance of evil and vileness, both within and without, there is an indefinable, inexpressible purpose central within all life.

> There is that in me—I do not know what it is—
> but I know it is in me.
>
> Wrench'd and sweaty—calm and cool then my
> body becomes,
> I sleep—I sleep long.
>
> I do not know it—it is without name—it is a word
> unsaid,
> It is not in any dictionary, utterance, symbol.
>
> Something it swings on more than the earth I
> swing on,
> To it the creation is the friend whose embracing
> awakes me.
> Perhaps I might tell more. Outlines ! I plead
> for my brothers and sisters.
>
> Do you see O my brothers and sisters ?
> is not chaos or death—it is form, union, plan—
> it is eternal life—it is Happiness.

He acknowledges, but does not apologize for his contradictions, his inconsequence. He is no more tame than a hawk. He cannot be translated into other terms than his own. He is hardly to be understood, but in so far as he is assimilated he will prove to be stamina and health.

Such, in bald, unsatisfying outline, is the "Song of Myself," the longest of Whitman's poems, which would fill about seventy pages of this book. On its first appearance it had no title other than that of the volume; nor, indeed, had any of the eleven succeeding chants. In 1856 the first was called "Poem of Walt Whitman, an American," then "Walt Whitman," and after 1876, "Song of Myself." The shorter pendent poems are now known as "A Song for Occupations," "To Think of Time," "The Sleepers," "I Sing the Body Electric," "Faces," "Song of the Answerer," "Europe," "A Boston Ballad (1854)," "There was a Child Went Forth," "Who Learns my Lesson Complete," and lastly, "Great are the Myths," only part of which now appears in "Leaves of Grass" as "Youth, Day, Old Age and Night."

"A Song for Occupations" declares the transcendental work of man, and the worth of any common man.

> We consider bibles and religions divine—I do not
> say they are not divine,
> I say they have all grown out of you, and may
> grow out of you still,
> It is not they who give the life, it is you who give
> the life,
> Leaves are not more shed from the trees, or trees
> from the earth, than they are shed out of you.

"To Think of Time" asserts the permanence

of personal identity, which death cannot dissolve. "The Sleepers," commencing,

> I wander all night in my visions,

suggests some more vivid experience than that of dreams. "Faces" gives, among many others, the portrait of his maternal grandmother :

> Behold a woman !
> She looks out from her quaker cap, her face is clearer and more beautiful than the sky.
>
> She sits in an armchair under the shaded porch of the farmhouse,
> The sun just shines on her old white head.
>
> Her ample gown is of cream-hued linen,
> Her grandsons raised the flax, and her granddaughters spun it with the distaff and the wheel.
>
> The melodious character of the earth,
> The finish beyond which philosophy cannot go and does not wish to go,
> The justified mother of men.

He sings "the Body Electric" with something of the spirit of a Renaissance painter, something of the Greek joy in the living statue. The splendour of the original poem was violated in 1856 by the addition of a superfluous page of specifications, an enumeration of physical details which fails to produce exhilaration. This cumulative method Whitman often employed, but rarely with success. Here is a passage from the earlier part :

I knew a man, a common farmer, the father of
five sons,
And in them the fathers of sons, and in them the
fathers of sons.
This man was of wonderful vigour, calmness,
beauty of person,
The shape of his head, the pale yellow and white
of his hair and beard, the immeasurable
meaning of his black eyes, the richness and
breadth of his manners,
These I used to go and visit him to see, he was
wise also,
He was six feet tall, he was over eighty years old,
his sons were massive, clean, bearded, tan-
faced, handsome,
They and his daughters loved him, all who saw
him loved him,
They did not love him by allowance, they loved
him with personal love,
He drank water only, the blood show'd like scarlet
through the clear-brown skin of his face,
He was a frequent gunner and fisher, he sail'd his
boat himself, he had a fine one presented to
him by a ship-joiner, he had fowling-pieces
presented to him by men that loved him,
When he went with his five sons and many
grand-sons to hunt or fish, you would pick
him out as the most beautiful and vigorous
of the gang,
You would wish long and long to be with him,
you would wish to sit by him in the boat
that you and he might touch each other.

And here is another :

Have you ever loved the body of a woman ?
Have you ever loved the body of a man ?

Do you not see that these are exactly the same to
all in all nations and times all over the earth ?

If anything is sacred the human body is sacred,
And the glory and sweet of a man is the token of
manhood untainted,
And in man or woman a clean, strong, firm-
fibred body is more beautiful than the most
beautiful face.

The "Song of the Answerer" as it now stands includes a part of the original prose preface, which broke up easily into loose rhythmical lines, not essentially different from the original poem. Indeed, by his absorption of a large part of the preface into the later editions of the chants, Whitman shows conclusively that his own nervous prose is not always to be distinguished from his poetry. The same kind of rhythm dominates each.

"Europe" and the "Boston Ballad" I have already referred to. "A Child went Forth" is largely, though not perhaps literally, autobiographical: the Quaker nomenclature for the months was introduced in 1860, immediately before he began writing his war-poems.

## THERE WAS A CHILD WENT FORTH

There was a child went forth every day,
And the first object he look'd upon, that object he
became,
And that object became part of him for the day
or a certain part of the day,
Or for many years or stretching cycles of years.

The early lilacs became part of this child,
And grass and white and red morning-glories, and white and red clover, and the song of the phœbe-bird,
And the Third-month lambs and the sow's pink-faint litter, and the mare's foal and the cow's calf,
And the noisy brood of the barnyard or by the mire of the pondside,
And the fish suspending themselves so curiously below there, and the beautiful curious liquid,
And the water-plants with their graceful flat heads, all became part of him.

The field-sprouts of Fourth-month and Fifth-month became part of him,
Winter-grain sprouts and those of the light-yellow corn, and the esculent roots of the garden,
And the apple-trees cover'd with blossoms and the fruit afterward, and wood-berries, and the commonest weeds by the road,
And the old drunkard staggering home from the outhouse of the tavern whence he had lately risen,
And the schoolmistress that pass'd on her way to the school,
And the friendly boys that pass'd, and the quarrelsome boys,
And the tidy and fresh-cheek'd girls, and the barefoot negro boy and girl,
And all the changes of city and country wherever he went.

His own parents, he that had father'd him and she that had conceiv'd him in her womb and birth'd him,

They gave this child more of themselves than that,
They gave him afterward every day, they became part of him.

The mother at home quietly placing the dishes on the supper-table,
The mother with mild words, clean her cap and gown, a wholesome odour falling off her person and clothes as she walks by,
The father, strong, self-sufficient, manly, mean, anger'd, unjust,
The blow, the quick loud word, the tight bargain, the crafty lure,
The family usages, the language, the company, the furniture, the yearning and swelling heart,
Affection that will not be gainsay'd, the sense of what is real, the thought if after all it should prove unreal,
The doubts of day-time and the doubts of night-time, the curious whether and how,
Whether that which appears so is so, or is it all flashes and specks ?
Men and women crowding fast in the streets, if they are not flashes and specks what are they ?
The streets themselves and the façades of houses, and goods in the windows,
Vehicles, teams, the heavy-plank'd wharves, the huge crossing at the ferries,
The village on the highland seen from afar at sunset, the river between,
Shadows, aureola and mist, the light falling on roofs and gables of white or brown two miles off,
The schooner near by sleepily dropping down the tide, the little boat slack-tow'd astern,

The hurrying tumbling waves, quick-broken crests, slapping,
The strata of colour'd clouds, the long bar of maroon-tint away solitary by itself, the spread of purity it lies motionless in,
The horizon's edge, the flying sea-crow, the fragrance of salt marsh and shore mud,
These became part of that child who went forth every day, and who now goes, and will always go forth every day.

Whitman is at his most naïve and crude in "Who Learns my Lesson." But "Great are the Myths" contains these splendid lines:

Youth, large, lusty, loving—youth full of grace, force, fascination,
Do you know that Old Age may come after you with equal grace, force, fascination?

Day full-blown and splendid—day of the immense sun, action, ambition, laughter,
The Night follows close with millions of suns, and sleep and restoring darkness.

Reviewing the first-fruits of Whitman's inspiration, we are almost overwhelmed by its originality, so markedly different in character from any contemporary work, even from Emerson's. Their author had turned right away from his early methods, from studies after Hawthorne and verses in the New England manner, to give expression to the America he himself knew best—that amazingly assimilative, expansive, and (we may now say it without offence) that self-conscious youth among the nations. Intellectually splendid and spiritually exhilarating as was the Emersonian message, the contribution of Thoreau, Whittier, Bryant, Longfellow, Lowell, and the rest, it lacked body and red blood. Whitman was impelled to supply this lack. His book is so charged with emotional dynamic as to be often only half-articulate. But another, a secondary, yet emphatic impression, conflicts strangely with the first: an impression of breaks in the spontaneity, of gesturing, of writing to a programme as the poet of the New York democracy, of self-assertions unworthy of a man who has entered the One Life wherein is neither great nor small. The fact remains that, with these obvious faults, the huge waves of undeniable inspiration sweep on, and nothing of failure is able finally to obscure their majestic power.

## IV

NO one has been more felicitously photographed than Whitman from 1854 onward. Of two daguerreotypes dating from that year, the one reproduced in "Leaves of Grass" represents him grave and challenging, wearing a soft wide-awake and artisan's blouse and trousers. In the other he is bareheaded and smiling, his rough black hair and short beard already grey at thirty-five—partly, no doubt, from constant sun and sea-bathing—the face absolutely radiant with vitality. Anyone who looks into the eyes of this remarkable portrait sees for himself the express image of that "friendly and flowing savage" by whom people of every class were attracted as to an 'answerer.' If he should not seem such to the present-day beholder, the latter must mentally set this portrait against its proper background, put this text back into its human context, the America of the poems. Then I think he will realize its significance. To that America belongs this open-hearted includer of all, this cosmic catholic; this self-discovered manhood, adventurously irresponsible in the enjoyment of all its scope and prerogative; this infectious extravagance of masculine vitality. Remember how hugely and irresponsibly America herself was growing: how ample and full her life, how pregnant with nebulous promise. Remember the unspoiled youthful idealism, the immense optimism of that second generation of Americans—the narrow colonial days, the hard struggles into political independence, left well behind, and now the intoxicating awakening to its own vast present, its vaster future. What incredible world-achievement awaited America! For in the fifties she stood already for man's will to be full-statured and independent; and felt herself able to make full-statured, independent citizens of the castaways, derelicts, and rejected of the Old World. She welcomed all, gave harbourage and opportunity to all, without any doubt of her assimilative power.

I do not say there is nothing repellent in this

face, and that America. It is yet crude, it conceals a weakness in its strength. It does not yet fully know itself. It is apt to be too "friendly and flowing." To us especially, with our dangerous habits of reserve, our masked faces, the lack of reticence here may seem shocking. It boasts too little delicacy, too little patience with the subtle and the slow. It is frank and primitive, as the Elizabethans were, though in a different kind. It is the symbol of that wholesome egoism, that aggressive physical splendour proper to the early life of a new people :—and is humanity yet so old, yet so accomplished as to its prime purpose, that it should outgrow this quality ? There is an aspect of Whitman's nature still unexpressed in all this. The fiery experience of supreme self-expression is yet far from complete for him. The war and its service was yet to come.

While the publication of his book emphasized his membership in the world of the 'average man,' a world out of which he never suffered himself to be transplanted, it brought Whitman new and notable literary friends. It was at Pfaff's Broadway restaurant that, as a member or associate of the Bohemian group of men and women, journalists, artists, and actors, who met there, he made the acquaintance of W. D. Howells and others ; but it was at his mother's house that Thoreau, Alcott and Emerson, Ward Beecher, Lord Houghton and Moncure Conway called upon him. Emerson's visit had been preceded by that letter which was in itself the principal tangible response to his venture.

Concord, Mass'tts., July 21st, 1855

Dear Sir,—I am not blind to the worth of the wonderful gift of "Leaves of Grass." I find it the most extraordinary piece of wit and wisdom that America has yet contributed. I am very happy in reading it, as great power makes us happy. It meets the demand I am always making of what seems the sterile and stingy nature, as if too much handiwork, or too much lymph in the temperament, were making our Western wits fat and mean. I give you joy of your free and brave thought. I have great joy in it. I find incomparable things said incomparably well, as they must be. I find the courage of treatment that so delights us and which large perception only can inspire.

I greet you at the beginning of a great career, which yet must have had a long foreground somewhere, for such a start. I rubbed my eyes a little, to see if this sunbeam were no illusion ; but the solid sense of the book is a sober certainty. It has the best merits, namely, of fortifying and encouraging.

I did not know until I last night saw the book advertised in a newspaper that I could trust the name as real and available for a post office. I wish to see my benefactor, and have felt much like striking my tasks and visiting New York to pay you my respects.

R. W. EMERSON

Mr. Walter Whitman

Here Emerson unfalteringly acclaims the new writer. Yet I think he is somewhat baffled by what in anyone younger we should not hesitate to call immaturities ; and he obviously suspects that "Walt Whitman" is somebody's pseudonym. With all the affinity and affection between these two great natures some barrier seemed to rise up between them: they never seem to have felt themselves at home together. Perhaps Whitman only half responded to the older man's advances. Yet for him Emerson's verdict easily outweighed the less favourable voices of others; and even if the magisterial tone was soon less certain, his first thought retains for us, too, its splendid and characteristic validity. Whittier burnt his copy of the poems in his stove; Lowell shook his head over their lack of restraint. But the critics were not all hostile: several notable voices spoke frankly in approval of the freshness and reality of the book, exculpating its author from any vicious taint or meretricious purpose.

Whitman himself contributed notices to several friendly papers: a form of advertisement in doubtful taste, though hardly more flagrant than the usual inspired paragraphs. More serious lapses from dignity may, however, be found in the enlarged second edition (of 1856)—bearing on its cover the words, "I greet you at the beginning of a great career. R. W. Emerson," and containing in an appendix to the poems an effusive, and on his own showing a misleading reply, unworthy of an honest salesman. It betrayed the defect of his quality, a certain childishness that alternated with his large and virile faith; a self-complacence that was sometimes an ugly ignorance of personal defects, which he never wholly outgrew. With all its faults, however (and the worst are withdrawn from subsequent issues), this edition is notable for its new poems: the "Song at Sunset," the "Songs" of "the Open Road," "the Rolling Earth," and "the Broad Axe," and "Crossing Brooklyn Ferry" (here called "Sundown Poem"). The original preface as such disappears, parts of it being reproduced in "By Blue Ontario's Shore," "Song of the Answerer," and "Song of Prudence."

The "Open Road" is perhaps the most widely known of Whitman's longer poems. It is full of courage, sanity, comradeship, and the open air ; and behind its brave, free cadences lurks much that does not appear at a first or second reading.

## SONG OF THE OPEN ROAD

1

Afoot and light-hearted I take to the open road,
Healthy, free, the world before me,
The long brown path before me leading wherever
    I choose.

Henceforth I ask not good-fortune, I myself am
    good-fortune,
Henceforth I whimper no more, postpone no more,
    need nothing,
Done with indoor complaints, libraries, querulous
    criticisms,
Strong and content I travel the open road.

The earth, that is sufficient,
I do not want the constellations any nearer,

I know they are very well where they are,
I know they suffice for those who belong to them.

(Still here I carry my old delicious burdens,
I carry them, men and women, I carry them with
me wherever I go,
I swear it is impossible for me to get rid of them,
I am fill'd with them, and I will fill them in return.)

2

You road I enter upon and look around, I believe
you are not all that is here,
I believe that much unseen is also here.

Here the profound lesson of reception, nor preference nor denial,
The black with his woolly head, the felon, the
diseas'd, the illiterate person, are not denied ;
The birth, the hasting after the physician, the
beggar's tramp, the drunkard's stagger, the
laughing party of mechanics,
The escaped youth, the rich person's carriage,
the fop, the eloping couple,
The early market-man, the hearse, the moving of
furniture into the town, the return back from
the town,
They pass, I also pass, any thing passes, none can
be interdicted,
None but are accepted, none but shall be dear to
me.

3

You air that serves me with breath to speak !
You objects that call from diffusion my meanings
and give them shape !

You light that wraps me and all things in delicate equable showers !
You paths worn in the irregular hollows by the roadsides !
I believe you are latent with unseen existences, you are so dear to me.

You flagg'd walks of the cities ! you strong curbs at the edges !
You ferries ! you planks and posts of wharves ! you timber-lined sides ! you distant ships !
You rows of houses ! you window-pierc'd façades ! you roofs !
You porches and entrances ! you copings and iron guards !
You windows whose transparent shells might expose so much !
You doors and ascending steps ! you arches !
You gray stones of interminable pavements ! you trodden crossings !
From all that has touch'd you I believe you have imparted to yourselves, and now would impart the same secretly to me,
From the living and the dead you have peopled your impassive surfaces, and the spirits thereof would be evident and amicable with me.

4

The earth expanding right hand and left hand,
The picture alive, every part in its best light,
The music falling in where it is wanted, and stopping where it is not wanted,
The cheerful voice of the public road, the gay fresh sentiment of the road.

O highway I travel, do you say to me *Do not leave me?*
Do you say *Venture not—if you leave me you are lost?*
Do you say *I am already prepared, I am well-beaten and undenied, adhere to me?*

O public road, I say back I am not afraid to leave you, yet I love you,
You express me better than I can express myself,
You shall be more to me than my poem.

I think heroic deeds were all conceiv'd in the open air, and all free poems also,
I think I could stop here myself and do miracles,
I think whatever I shall meet on the road I shall like, and whoever beholds me shall like me,
I think whoever I see must be happy.

5

From this hour I ordain myself loos'd of limits and imaginary lines,
Going where I list, my own master total and absolute,
Listening to others, considering well what they say,
Pausing, searching, receiving, contemplating,
Gently, but with undeniable will, divesting myself of the holds that would hold me.

I inhale great draughts of space,
The east and the west are mine, and the north and the south are mine.

I am larger, better than I thought,
I did not know I held so much goodness.

All seems beautiful to me,

I can repeat over to men and women You have done such good to me I would do the same to you,
I will recruit for myself and you as I go,
I will scatter myself among men and women as I go,
I will toss a new gladness and roughness among them,
Whoever denies me it shall not trouble me,
Whoever accepts me he or she shall be blessed and shall bless me.

6

Now if a thousand perfect men were to appear it would not amaze me,
Now if a thousand beautiful forms of women appear'd it would not astonish me.

Now I see the secret of the making of the best persons,
It is to grow in the open air and to eat and sleep with the earth.

Here a great personal deed has room,
(Such a deed seizes upon the hearts of the whole race of men,
Its effusion of strength and will overwhelms law and mocks all authority and all argument against it.)

Here is the test of wisdom,
Wisdom is not finally tested in schools,
Wisdom cannot be pass'd from one having it to another not having it,
Wisdom is of the soul, is not susceptible of proof, is its own proof,

Applies to all stages and objects and qualities and
is content,
Is the certainty of the reality and immortality of
things, and the excellence of things ;
Something there is in the float of the sight of
things that provokes it out of the soul.

Now I re-examine philosophies and religions,
They may prove well in lecture-rooms, yet not
prove at all under the spacious clouds and
along the landscape and flowing currents.
Here is realization,
Here is a man tallied—he realizes here what he
has in him,
The past, the future, majesty, love—if they are
vacant of you, you are vacant of them.

Only the kernel of every object nourishes ;
Where is he who tears off the husks for you and
me ?
Where is he that undoes stratagems and envelopes
for you and me ?

Here is adhesiveness, it is not previously fashion'd,
it is apropos ;
Do you know what it is as you pass to be loved by
strangers ?
Do you know the talk of those turning eye-balls ?

7

Here is the efflux of the soul,
The efflux of the soul comes from within through
embower'd gates, ever provoking questions,
These yearnings why are they ? these thoughts in
the darkness why are they ?

Why are there men and women that while they are nigh me the sunlight expands my blood ?
Why when they leave me do my pennants of joy sink flat and lank ?
Why are there trees I never walk under but large and melodious thoughts descend upon me ?
(I think they hang there winter and summer on those trees and always drop fruit as I pass ;)
What is it I interchange so suddenly with strangers ?
What with some driver as I ride on the seat by his side ?
What with some fisherman drawing his seine by the shore as I walk by and pause ?
What gives me to be free to a woman's and man's good-will ? what gives them to be free to mine ?

8

The efflux of the soul is happiness, here is happiness,
I think it pervades the open air, waiting at all times,
Now it flows unto us, we are rightly charged.

Here rises the fluid and attaching character,
The fluid and attaching character is the freshness and sweetness of man and woman,
(The herbs of the morning sprout no fresher and sweeter every day out of the roots of themselves, than it sprouts fresh and sweet continually out of itself.)

Toward the fluid and attaching character exudes the sweat of the love of young and old,
From it falls distill'd the charm that mocks beauty and attainments,

Toward it heaves the shuddering longing ache of
contact.

9

Allons! whoever you are come travel with me!
Travelling with me you find what never tires.

The earth never tires,
The earth is rude, silent, incomprehensible at first,
Nature is rude and incomprehensible at first,
Be not discouraged, keep on, there are divine
things well envelop'd,
I swear to you there are divine things more
beautiful than words can tell.

Allons! we must not stop here,
However sweet these laid-up stores, however convenient this dwelling we cannot remain here,
However shelter'd this port and however calm
these waters we must not anchor here,
However welcome the hospitality that surrounds
us we are permitted to receive it but a little
while.

10

Allons! the inducements shall be greater,
We will sail pathless and wild seas,
We will go where winds blow, waves dash, and the
Yankee clipper speeds by under full sail.

Allons! with power, liberty, the earth, the
elements,
Health, defiance, gayety, self-esteem, curiosity;
Allons! from all formules!
From your formules, O bat-eyed and materialistic
priests.

The stale cadaver blocks up the passage—the
burial waits no longer.

Allons! yet take warning!
He travelling with me needs the best blood, thews, endurance,
None may come to the trial till he or she bring courage and health,
Come not here if you have already spent the best of yourself,
Only those may come who come in sweet and determin'd bodies,
No diseas'd person, no rum-drinker or venereal taint is permitted here.

(I and mine do not convince by arguments, similes, rhymes,
We convince by our presence.)

II

Listen! I will be honest with you,
I do not offer the old smooth prizes, but offer rough new prizes,
These are the days that must happen to you:
You shall not heap up what is call'd riches,
You shall scatter with lavish hand all that you earn or achieve,
You but arrive at the city to which you were destin'd, you hardly settle yourself to satisfaction before you are call'd by an irresistible call to depart,
You shall be treated to the ironical smiles and mockings of those who remain behind you,
What beckonings of love you receive you shall only answer with passionate kisses of parting,
You shall not allow the hold of those who spread their reach'd hands toward you.

12

Allons! after the great Companions, and to belong to them!
They too are on the road—they are the swift and majestic men—they are the greatest women,
Enjoyers of calms of seas and storms of seas,
Sailors of many a ship, walkers of many a mile of land,
Habituès of many distant countries, habituès of far-distant dwellings,
Trusters of men and women, observers of cities, solitary toilers,
Pausers and contemplators of tufts, blossoms, shells of the shore,
Dancers at wedding-dances, kissers of brides, tender helpers of children, bearers of children,
Soldiers of revolts, standers by gaping graves, lowerers-down of coffins,
Journeyers over consecutive seasons, over the years, the curious years each emerging from that which preceded it,
Journeyers as with companions, namely their own diverse phases,
Forth-steppers from the latent unrealized baby-days,
Journeyers gayly with their own youth, journeyers with their bearded and well-grain'd manhood,
Journeyers with their womanhood, ample, unsurpass'd, content,
Journeyers with their own sublime old age of manhood or womanhood,
Old age, calm, expanded, broad with the haughty breadth of the universe,

Old age, flowing free with the delicious near-by
freedom of death.

13

Allons! to that which is endless as it was beginningless,
To undergo much, tramps of days, rests of nights,
To merge all in the travel they tend to, and the days and nights they tend to,
Again to merge them in the start of superior journeys,
To see nothing anywhere but what you may reach it and pass it,
To conceive no time, however distant, but what you may reach it and pass it,
To look up or down no road but it stretches and waits for you, however long but it stretches and waits for you.
To see no being, not God's or any, but you also go thither,
To see no possession but you may possess it, enjoying all without labour or purchase, abstracting the feast yet not abstracting one particle of it,
To take the best of the farmer's farm and the rich man's elegant villa, and the chaste blessings of the well-married couple, and the fruits of orchards and flowers of gardens,
To take to your use out of the compact cities as you pass through,
To carry buildings and streets with you afterward wherever you go,
To gather the minds of men out of their brains as you encounter them, to gather the love out of their hearts,

To take your lovers on the road with you, for all
that you leave them behind you,
To know the universe itself as a road, as many
roads, as roads for travelling souls.

All parts away for the progress of souls,
All religion, all solid things, arts, governments—
all that was or is apparent upon this globe
or any globe, falls into niches and corners
before the procession of souls along the grand
roads of the universe.

Of the progress of the souls of men and women
along the grand roads of the universe, all
other progress is the needed emblem and
sustenance.

Forever alive, forever forward,
Stately, solemn, sad, withdrawn, baffled, mad,
turbulent, feeble, dissatisfied,
Desperate, proud, fond, sick, accepted by men,
rejected by men,
They go ! they go ! I know that they go, but I
know not where they go,
But I know that they go toward the best—toward
something great.

Whoever you are, come forth ! or man or woman
come forth !
You must not stay sleeping and dallying there in
the house, though you built it, or though it
has been built for you.

Out of the dark confinement ! out from behind the
screen !
It is useless to protest, I know all and expose
it.

Behold through you as bad as the rest,
Through the laughter, dancing, dining, supping, of people,
Inside of dresses and ornaments, inside of those wash'd and trimm'd faces,
Behold a secret silent loathing and despair.

No husband, no wife, no friend, trusted to hear the confession,
Another self, a duplicate of every one, skulking and hiding it goes,
Formless and wordless through the streets of the cities, polite and bland in the parlours,
In the cars of railroads, in steamboats, in the public assembly,
Home to the houses of men and women, at the table, in the bed-room, everywhere,
Smartly attired, countenance smiling, form upright, death under the breast-bones, hell under the skull-bones,
Under the broadcloth and gloves, under the ribbons and artificial flowers,
Keeping fair with the customs, speaking not a syllable of itself,
Speaking of any thing else but never of itself.

14

Allons ! through struggles and wars !
The goal that was named cannot be countermanded.

Have the past struggles succeeded ?
What has succeeded ? yourself ? your nation ? Nature ?
Now understand me well—it is provided in the essence of things that from any fruition of

success, no matter what, shall come forth something to make a greater struggle necessary.

My call is the call of battle, I nourish active rebellion,
He going with me must go well arm'd,
He going with me goes often with spare diet, poverty, angry enemies, desertions.

15

Allons ! the road is before us !
It is safe—I have tried it—my own feet have tried it well—be not detain'd !
Let the paper remain on the desk unwritten, and the book on the shelf unopen'd !
Let the tools remain in the workshop ! let the money remain unearn'd !
Let the school stand ! mind not the cry of the teacher !
Let the preacher preach in his pulpit ! let the lawyer plead in the court, and the judge expound the law.

Camerado, I give you my hand !
I give you my love more precious than money,
I give you myself before preaching or law ;
Will you give me yourself ? will you come travel with me ?
Shall we stick by each other as long as we live ?

The "Song of the Broad-Axe" opens with curious staccato rhymes:

Fingers of the organist skipping staccato over the keys of the great organ

—an effect as of the dripping of rain.

Weapon shapely, naked, wan,
Head from the mother's bowels drawn,
Wooded flesh and metal bone, limb only one and
    lip only one,
Grey-blue leaf by red-heat grown, helve produced
    from a little seed sown,
Resting the grass amid and upon,
To be lean'd and to lean on.

Note the curious flattened ending, a device Whitman often used. The poem offers the axe as an emblem to America ; and suggests in bold panorama those outstanding generous types of active man and womanhood that Whitman regarded as characteristic of her. But panorama deteriorates into enumeration with showers and volleys of nouns. Deliberately essayed as a new artistic method after the manner of Homer's catalogues of ships and captains, it produces on many readers an effect like that of the hoardings covered with advertisements that one passes in the train, an effect rather distracting than suggestive. But Whitman, with his love of exhibitions and similar aggregations of objects, does not seem to have disliked this kind of sensation at all ; he enjoyed and sought to reproduce it. I confess I do not ; but I cannot leave this poem without quoting its famous description of free womanhood :

Her shape arises,
She less guarded than ever, yet more guarded
    than ever,
The gross and soil'd she moves among do not
    make her gross and soil'd,

She knows the thoughts as she passes, nothing is
 conceal'd from her,
She is none the less considerate or friendly
 therefor,
She is the best belov'd, it is without exception,
 she has no reason to fear and she does not
 fear,
Oaths, quarrels, hiccupp'd songs, smutty expres-
 sions, are idle to her as she passes,
She is silent, she is possess'd of herself, they do
 not offend her,
She receives them as the laws of Nature receive
 them, she is strong,
She too is a law of Nature—there is no law
 stronger than she is.

Whitman's canticle of the sun may profitably be compared with the different and yet kindred song of St. Francis. Such comparison would reveal the distance that intervenes between two ages of faith.

## SONG AT SUNSET

Splendour of ended day floating and filling me,
Hour prophetic, hour resuming the past,
Inflating my throat, you divine average,
You earth and life till the last ray gleams I sing.

Open mouth of my soul uttering gladness,
Eyes of my soul seeing perfection,
Natural life of me faithfully praising things,
Corroborating forever the triumph of things.

Illustrious every one !
Illustrious what we name space, sphere of un-
 number'd spirits,

Illustrious the mystery of motion in all beings,
even the tiniest insect,
Illustrious the attribute of speech, the senses, the
body,
Illustrious the passing light—illustrious the pale
reflection on the new moon in the western sky,
Illustrious whatever I see or hear or touch, to the
last.

Good in all,
In the satisfaction and aplomb of animals,
In the annual return of the seasons,
In the hilarity of youth,
In the strength and flush of manhood,
In the grandeur and exquisiteness of old age,
In the superb vistas of death.

Wonderful to depart!
Wonderful to be here!
The heart, to jet the all-alike and innocent blood!
To breathe the air, how delicious!
To speak—to walk—to seize something by the
hand!
To prepare for sleep, for bed, to look on my rose-
colour'd flesh!
To be conscious of my body, so satisfied, so large!
To be this incredible God I am!
To have gone forth among other Gods, these men
and women I love.

Wonderful how I celebrate you and myself!
How my thoughts play subtly at the spectacles
around!
How the clouds pass silently overhead!
How the earth darts on and on! and how the sun,
moon, stars, dart on and on!

How the water sports and sings ! (surely it is alive!)
How the trees rise and stand up, with strong trunks, with branches and leaves !
(Surely there is something more in each of the trees, some living soul.)

O amazement of things—even the least particle !
O spirituality of things !
O strain musical flowing through ages and continents, now reaching me and America !
I take your strong chords, intersperse them, and cheerfully pass them forward.

I too carol the sun, usher'd or at noon, or as now, setting,
I too throb to the brain and beauty of the earth and of all the growths of the earth,
I too have felt the resistless call of myself.

As I steam'd down the Mississippi,
As I wander'd over the prairies,
As I have lived, as I have look'd through my windows my eyes,
As I went forth in the morning, as I beheld the light breaking in the east,
As I bathed on the beach of the Eastern Sea, and again on the beach of the Western Sea,
As I roam'd the streets of inland Chicago, whatever streets I have roam'd,
Or cities or silent woods, or even amid the sights of war,
Wherever I have been I have charged myself with contentment and triumph.

I sing to the last the equalities modern or old,
I sing the endless finalés of things,
I say Nature continues, glory continues,

I praise with electric voice,
For I do not see one imperfection in the universe,
And I do not see one cause or result lamentable
at last in the universe.

O setting sun ! though the time has come,
I still warble under you, if none else does, unmitigated adoration.

The "Poem of Many in One" (which later, with additions and alterations, became "By Blue Ontario's Shore") is a veritable democratic manifesto, with its notable cries,

Produce great persons, the rest follows,

and

O America, because you build for mankind I build for you !

"Democratic Vistas" afterwards took up the same theme, treating it more fully though not more forcefully.

In the "Song of the Rolling Earth" the idea of progress and amelioration is broadly and profoundly suggested, but I cannot attempt to summarize its meaning here. In several of the new poems Whitman seeks to spur young America out of sin and sloth to meet its high destiny. He continually asserts the glory of health, of full manhood and a magnetic personality. The soul is immortal, but the body we build up by our way of living gives proportions to that soul, capacitating or incapacitating it for its life in other spheres :

I do not know how, but I know it is so.

This conception also underlies his poems of sex. Somehow, human life is inextricably bound up, especially at certain critical stages, with sex. To live, in any absolute sense, is to give expression to the spirit ; and in this sex has its urgent part. Whitman was not merely a eugenist—he would have urged revolt against some eugenistic doctrines—his great difference from his New England friends lay in his attitude toward passion. It was not something to be apologized for, or merely etherealized. His attitude toward passion is bound up with his attitude toward women, who are always in his pages the equals and comrades of men. Womanhood is at least as absolute and final a term for Whitman as manhood, and is as divine. He believed that the glorification of paternity would result in a humanization of all relations between men and women, with consequent new reaches of freedom for the whole race.

Let us recall that it was after reading this edition that Thoreau wrote to a friend :

That Walt Whitman, of whom I wrote to you, is the most interesting fact to me at present. I have just read his second edition (which he gave me), and it has done me more good than any reading for a long time. Perhaps I remember best the poem of Walt Whitman, an American, and the Sun-down Poem. There are two or three pieces in the book which are disagreeable, to say the least ; simply sensual. He does not celebrate love at all. It is as if the beasts spoke. . . . But even on this side he has spoken more truth than any American or modern that I know. I have found his poem exhilarating, encouraging. . . . On the whole, it sounds to me very brave and American, after whatever deductions. I do not believe that all the sermons, so called, that have been preached in this land, put together, are equal to it for preaching. . . . Though rude, and sometimes ineffectual, it is a great primitive poem—an alarum or trumpet-note ringing through the American camp. Wonderfully like the Orientals, too, considering that when I asked him if he had read them, he answered, "No: tell me about them." . . . Since I have seen him, I find that I am not disturbed by any brag or egoism in his book. He may turn out the least of a braggart of all, having a better right to be confident. He is a great fellow.

With this remarkable tribute from one of the ablest and finest intelligences of the day should be read the following sentences regarding the poems specially criticized by Thoreau, written by an Englishwoman, Mrs. Anne Gilchrist, a dozen years later (1869):

In regard to those poems which raised so loud an outcry, I will take courage to say frankly that I find them also beautiful. . . . Perhaps, indeed, they were chiefly written for wives. I rejoice to have read these poems; and if I, or any true woman, feel that, certainly *men* may hold their peace about them. You will understand that I still think that instinct of silence I spoke of, a right and beautiful thing; and that it is only lovers and poets (perhaps only lovers and *this* poet) who may say what they will. . . .

The root of Whitman's treatment of evil is found in "This Compost." The earth, accepting man's vilest leavings, converts them, by its chemistry, into the materials of beauty and health. Such, the poet indicates, is the chemistry of the human spirit, similarly able to accept all experience. The analogy can only be seized as a suggestion; and even as a suggestion is open to serious misunderstanding. As the earth transforms morbidity into wholesomeness, so also does the spirit of man. But the transformation is due to an active process and principle, a process of assimilation:

> What chemistry! . . .
> It grows such sweet things out of such corruptions. . . .

This 'chemistry' obviously requires a right active relation to the material to be assimilated, a relation in nowise fulfilled by any form of slovenly or evil living.

In the light of this poem, let us look again at the criticism suggested in Thoreau's sentence, "It is as if the beasts spoke," which applies with even greater force to certain passages in the edition of 1860. Altogether apart from Thoreau's personal attitude, which lacks the broad base of Whitman's great faith, I find a measure of justification for his demur. Not, indeed, in Whitman's faith, nor in his frank acceptance of the organism of passion, but in a confusion of thought with regard to the sources of inspiration. Thus when he declares:

> I harbour for good or bad, I permit to speak at
> every hazard,
> Nature, without check, with original energy,

he betrays, in his use of the vague word 'nature,' a weakness of intellectual grip on the character of inspiration and the dangers besetting it. If it be a poet's habit to abandon himself to any vagrant emotion that may seek him out, his inspiration will sooner or later fail of those higher sanctions Whitman sought. Irruptions from low sensational levels are all too common in the world of art, as elsewhere. They are hostile to Whitman's clearly declared purpose; yet a romantic and misleading use of the term 'nature,' common among optimists, permitted him at times to regard such irruptions with mischievous complacency. This jumps with a certain lack of discrimination as regards his true self. There were times when his theory of expression was simply to let himself go, anyhow, and whatever his mood—"if I felt like the devil, to say so." Surely this is a parody of that perfect faith which refuses to reject any of the elements of life. Such faith is inseparably bound up with the exercise of vital choice. It does not merely lie open to 'nature,' but selects, even if half-unconsciously, the material it needs, and can therefore assimilate, for its utterance.

Expression of his inner realization is the poet's gift to the world. In so far as Whitman, having glimpsed the purpose and plan implicit in progress, gave utterance to that, he nobly fulfilled his function and his own conception of it. When, however, he gives his human voice "without check, with original energy," to those crude forces in man which are not yet humanized, he seems to me to mistake and even to abuse it. But such occasions are rare.

Inspiration has dangers that those who never experience it can hardly realize. We may only abandon ourselves to that which we know to be higher than ourselves, and so divine. Any other self-abandonment involves a betrayal, a harking back to the beast, and offers an opportunity to the baser elements.

While Whitman's wholesome and positive nature, and above all his profound purpose, kept him from really confusing licence with freedom, I think he did not sufficiently realize the danger for his message of the *laissez-faire* position he occasionally assumed. We are safe from misunderstanding him so long as we keep hold of the central principle of his life and work, his ultimate, ever-present faith. His was no rudderless boat adrift on the tide. Behind his sensuous optimism, his naturally happy disposition, his affectionate temperament and consummate physical and mental health, behind these to balance them, often unexpressed by him, but always present, was the huge driving force of his conscious will and purpose. In that lay his truly American, assimilative power. He celebrates America because of her august purpose. He discovers not only democracy in her, but personality which depends on purpose;

and religion, beheld and conceived of her anew. It is true, the outer shows sometimes seduced him naïvely to vaunt the very extravagances of vitality; but even in the days before the war, when this mood was most frequent, even while he accepted the shadow and shame as part of the rich, crude life of New York, he realized the peril besetting his land. He never blinked the tremendous struggle that assimilation on such a scale involves; the ceaseless breeding of athlete wrestlers, resolute, determined sons and comrades, if the sleepless, threatening, treacherous powers of oppression and greed were to be held in check. He never forgot those, but he would not, by any formal recognition, accord them, as it were, belligerent rights. His America should have vital power to assimilate even slavery. For he held the Free-soil doctrine, as eventually enunciated by Lincoln, that if America ceased to create slave-territory the superior vitality of freedom in the free territory must inevitably outweigh and predominate over the slave power. The black stain, unable to spread, would tend to wear out. This doctrine is characteristic of Whitman's general attitude toward evil. He acknowledged its peril; but he so profoundly believed in the antiseptic virtue of life that he would consider no sin-cure save a robust faith. He would not parley with fear or remorse. He thought there had been too much of that already. His affair was with life, to fortify and assure that. I think that, like Lincoln, he must have recognized that an hour of mortal crisis might indeed come; for while he repudiated the Abolitionist position he had a certain sympathy for old John Brown. I think he knew that an evil spirit might so come to possess the body politic that its casting forth would be a matter not only for prayer and fasting, but of grievous tearing. And similar knowledge must have come to him with regard to certain forms of individual sin. For better and worse, however, he deliberately ignored the virtue and vice of current individualist morality for the sake of what he regarded as a higher law. He sought to breathe a spirit into his readers that would carry them far out into life beyond merely egotistical preoccupations, into those high seas, those upland fields of personality, wherein man becomes at last a member of a free race endowed with a divine calling. For those who cannot respond to such an appeal Whitman's message must be ineffective; and if ineffective, it may easily become even noxious. This also he knew.

## V

FROM 1856 till the outbreak of the Southern rebellion Whitman continued his self-imposed task of creating a truly American attitude of mind. The need was urgent, and with the disappointing reception of his poems his mind turned to other channels of expression if he might thereby achieve his end. He proposed to undertake a national propaganda as orator and lecturer. With a noble conception of the orator's art corresponding closely to that of the poet, he lacked, however, the essential instrument, a magnetic voice. The post of 'Champion of America,' which he coveted, fell to a man not less worthy and better qualified. And perhaps, with the emergence, just at this time, of Abraham Lincoln from the Eighth Illinois Circuit into public view, Whitman may have felt the pressure of this claim less heavy. However that may be, for several years he still nursed the fancy of eking out his livelihood and furthering the supreme purpose of his life by peripatetic lecturing, a fancy into which I do not doubt a certain element of personal vanity contrived to enter. Occasionally in his later years, especially on the anniversaries of Lincoln's assassination, he would gather an audience around him.

Save for a visit to Boston, and it may be some excursions to the South, he pursued meanwhile his Brooklyn life; frequenting more than ever, if that were possible, Ferry and crowded Broadway, with solitary interludes on the then deserted Coney Island beach. Close friendship became increasingly necessary to him; and this he seems to have sought rather among stage-drivers and boat-hands than among his literary acquaintance. In the pursuit of these friendships he paid frequent visits to the hospital wards, and, perhaps, prison cells, whither mischief or mischance frequently brought those bold fellows. We are able to follow such a friendship, a few years later, in Whitman's letters to the Washington tram-conductor, Peter Doyle. It was on similar errands of natural affection that he commenced his visits to the war hospitals. If he was a friend of Emerson, and a frequenter of Pfaff's, he felt himself essentially a country-born, working-class man, and was intensely conservative in his personal habits. This is emphatically asserted in the 1860 "Leaves of Grass," which, though issued in Boston, might justly be described as "the arrogant Manhattanese" edition. It wore a splendid orange coat, and carried a real publisher's name on its beflourished title-page. Ill-fortune soon overtook it. A year after its appearance, on the outbreak of the war, the publishers came to wreck; the plates were sold off, and fell into the hands of a trader who gave Whitman no share in his own considerable profit.

This 1860 volume contains rather more than half of the complete poems, built into an organic scheme. Beside the enlarged group of "Children of Adam," with its beautiful prelude and epilogue, the most important of the new poems are the "Calamus" group, and the great chant "Out of the Cradle," whose sustained dignity was never violated by those aggressive Bohemianisms that for a time marked some of the pages of this edition till a maturer taste pruned them away.

# WHITMAN & HIS POETRY

## OUT OF THE CRADLE ENDLESSLY ROCKING

Out of the cradle endlessly rocking,
Out of the mocking-bird's throat, the musical shuttle,
Out of the Ninth-month midnight,
Over the sterile sands and the fields beyond, where the child leaving his bed wander'd alone, bareheaded, barefoot,
Down from the shower'd halo,
Up from the mystic play of shadows twining and twisting as if they were alive,
Out from the patches of briers and blackberries,
From the memories of the bird that chanted to me,
From your memories sad brother, from the fitful risings and fallings I heard,
From under that yellow half-moon late-risen and swollen as if with tears,
From those beginning notes of yearning and love there in the mist,
From the thousand responses of my heart never to cease,
From the myriad thence-arous'd words,
From the word stronger and more delicious than any,
From such as now they start the scene revisiting,
As a flock, twittering, rising, or overhead passing,
Borne hither, ere all eludes me, hurriedly,
A man, yet by these tears a little boy again,
Throwing myself on the sand, confronting the waves,
I, chanter of pains and joys, uniter of here and hereafter,
Taking all hints to use them, but swiftly leaping beyond them,
A reminiscence sing.

Once Paumanok,
When the lilac-scent was in the air and Fifth-month grass was growing,
Up this seashore in some briers,
Two feather'd guests from Alabama, two together,
And their nest, and four light-green eggs spotted with brown,
And every day the he-bird to and fro near at hand,
And every day the she-bird crouch'd on her nest, silent, with bright eyes,
And every day I, a curious boy, never too close, never disturbing them,
Cautiously peering, absorbing, translating.

*Shine ! shine ! shine !*
*Pour down your warmth, great sun*
*While we bask, we two together.*

*Two together !*
*Winds blow south, or winds blow north,*
*Day come white, or night come black,*
*Home, or rivers and mountains from home,*
*Singing all time, minding no time,*
*While we two keep together.*

Till of a sudden,
May-be kill'd, unknown to her mate,
One forenoon the she-bird crouch'd not on the nest,
Nor return'd that afternoon, nor the next,
Nor ever appear'd again.

And thenceforward all summer in the sound of the sea,
And at night under the full of the moon in calmer weather,
Over the hoarse surging of the sea,

Or flitting from brier to brier by day,
I saw, I heard at intervals the remaining one, the
he-bird,
The solitary guest from Alabama.

*Blow! blow! blow!*
*Blow up sea-winds along Paumanok's shore;*
*I wait and I wait till you blow my mate to me.*

Yes, when the stars glisten'd,
All night long on the prong of a moss-scallop'd
stake,
Down almost amid the slapping waves,
Sat the lone singer wonderful causing tears.

He call'd on his mate,
He pour'd forth the meanings which I of all men
know.

Yes my brother I know,
The rest might not, but I have treasur'd every
note,
For more than once dimly down to the beach
gliding,
Silent, avoiding the moonbeams, blending myself
with the shadows,
Recalling now the obscure shapes, the echoes, the
sounds and sights after their sorts,
The white arms out in the breakers tirelessly
tossing,
I, with bare feet, a child, the wind wafting my hair
Listen'd long and long.

Listen'd to keep, to sing, now translating the
notes,
Following you my brother.

*Soothe ! soothe ! soothe !*
*Close on its wave soothes the wave behind,*
*And again another behind embracing and lapping, every one close,*
*But my love soothes not me, not me.*

*Low hangs the moon, it rose late,*
*It is lagging—O I think it is heavy with love, with love.*

*O madly the sea pushes upon the land,*
*With love, with love.*

*O night ! do I not see my love fluttering out among the breakers ?*
*What is that little black thing I see there in the white ?*

*Loud ! loud ! loud !*
*Loud I call to you, my love !*
*High and clear I shoot my voice over the waves,*
*Surely you must know who is here, is here,*
*You must know who I am, my love.*

*Low-hanging moon !*
*What is that dusky spot in your brown yellow ?*
*O it is the shape, the shape of my mate !*
*O moon do not keep her from me any longer.*

*Land ! land ! O land !*
*Whichever way I turn, O I think you could give me my mate back again if you only would,*
*For I am almost sure I see her dimly whichever way I look.*

*O rising stars !*
*Perhaps the one I want so much will rise, will rise with some of you.*

*O throat! O trembling throat!*
*Sound clearer through the atmosphere!*
*Pierce the woods, the earth,*
*Somewhere listening to catch you must be the one I want.*

*Shake out carols!*
*Solitary here, the night's carols!*
*Carols of lonesome love! death's carols!*
*Carols under that lagging, yellow, waning moon!*
*O under that moon where she droops almost down into the sea!*
*O reckless despairing carols.*

*But soft! sink low!*
*Soft! let me just murmur,*
*And do you wait a moment you husky-nois'd sea,*
*For somewhere I believe I heard my mate responding to me,*
*So faint, I must be still, be still to listen,*
*But not altogether still, for then she might not come immediately to me.*

*Hither my love!*
*Here I am! here!*
*With this just-sustain'd note I announce myself to you,*
*This gentle call is for you my love, for you.*

*Do not be decoy'd elsewhere,*
*That is the whistle of the wind, it is not my voice,*
*That is the fluttering, the fluttering of the spray,*
*Those are the shadows of leaves.*

*O darkness! O in vain!*
*O I am very sick and sorrowful.*

*O brown halo in the sky near the moon, drooping upon the sea!*
*O troubled reflection in the sea!*
*O throat! O throbbing heart!*
*And I singing uselessly, uselessly all the night.*

*O past! O happy life! O songs of joy!*
*In the air, in the woods, over fields,*
*Loved! loved! loved! loved! loved!*
*But my mate no more, no more with me!*
*We two together no more.*

The aria sinking,
All else continuing, the stars shining,
The winds blowing, the notes of the bird continuous echoing,
With angry moans the fierce old mother incessantly moaning,
On the sands of Paumanok's shore gray and rustling,
The yellow half-moon enlarged, sagging down, drooping, the face of the sea almost touching,
The boy ecstatic, with his bare feet the waves, with his hair the atmosphere dallying,
The love in the heart long pent, now loose, now at last tumultuously bursting,
The aria's meaning, the ears, the soul, swiftly depositing,
The strange tears down the cheeks coursing,
The colloquy there, the trio, each uttering,
The undertone, the savage old mother incessantly crying,
To the boy's soul's questions sullenly timing, some drown'd secret hissing,
To the outsetting bard.

Demon or bird! (said the boy's soul),

Is it indeed toward your mate you sing? or is it
 really to me?
For I, that was a child, my tongue's use sleeping,
 now I have heard you,
Now in a moment I know what I am for, I awake,
And already a thousand singers, a thousand songs,
 clearer, louder and more sorrowful than yours,
A thousand warbling echoes have started to life
 within me, never to die.

O you singer solitary, singing by yourself, pro-
 jecting me,
O solitary me listening, never more shall I cease
 perpetuating you,
Never more shall I escape, never more the rever-
 berations,
Never more the cries of unsatisfied love be absent
 from me,
Never again leave me to be the peaceful child I
 was before what there in the night,
By the sea under the yellow and sagging moon,
The messenger there arous'd, the fire, the sweet
 hell within,
The unknown want, the destiny of me.

O give me the clew! (it lurks in the night here
 somewhere),
O if I am to have so much, let me have more

A word then, (for I will conquer it),
The word final, superior to all,
Subtle, sent up—what is it?—I listen;
Are you whispering it, and have been all the time,
 you sea-waves?
Is that it from your liquid rims and wet sands?

Whereto answering, the sea,

Delaying not, hurrying not,
Whisper'd me through the night, and very plainly
before daybreak,
Lisp'd to me the low and delicious word death,
And again death, death, death, death,
Hissing melodious, neither like the bird nor like
my arous'd child's heart,
But edging near as privately for me rustling at
my feet,
Creeping thence steadily up to my ears and laving
me softly all over,
Death, death, death, death, death.

Which I do not forget,
But fuse the song of my dusky demon and brother,
That he sang to me in the moonlight on Paumanok's gray beach,
With the thousand responsive songs at random,
My own songs awaked from that hour,
And with them the key, the word up from the waves,
The word of the sweetest song and all songs,
That strong and delicious word which, creeping to
my feet,
(Or like some old crone rocking the cradle, swathed
in sweet garments, bending aside),
The sea whisper'd me.

The "Calamus" poems are especially characteristic of Whitman, and I find it difficult to speak of them as briefly as here I must. Rightly understood, they would afford a key to much that is obscure and difficult in his work. But they are more easily misunderstood, for in truth they are enigmatic enough. They cannot be discussed alone. They have an organic relation to the rest of "Leaves of Grass"; to the "Song of Myself," with its cyclopean foundations of personal identity and prerogative; to "Children of Adam," inaugurating a new race of free persons; and to such poems of America—"the Mother of All," "the Many-in-One"—as "By Blue Ontario's Shores." For in "Calamus"—the name is that of a pond-side sedge—Whitman endeavours to suggest a passionate masculine communion of comradeship upon which social freedom might securely rest. Freedom of the individual alone, as exultantly sung in the "Song of Myself," does not provide a basis for a free society. Neither does the physical bond between the members of a family. The bond here demanded must be at once vital and liberating, an intimate attachment and a common purpose. Not only is such a fellowship the prerequisite of social freedom; personality itself requires it. Thus he writes in "In Paths Untrodden":

> In paths untrodden,
> In the growth by margins of pond-waters,
> Escaped from the life that exhibits itself,
> From all the standards hitherto publish'd, from
>     the pleasures, profits, conformities,
> Which too long I was offering to feed my soul,
> Clear to me now standards not yet publish'd,
>     clear to me that my soul,
> That the soul of the man I speak for rejoices in
>     comrades,
> Here by myself away from the clank of the world,
> Tallying and talk'd to here by tongues aromatic,

No longer abash'd, (for in this secluded spot I can
respond as I would not dare elsewhere),
Strong upon me the life that does not exhibit itself,
yet contains all the rest,
Resolv'd to sing no songs to-day but those of
manly attachment,
Projecting them along that substantial life,
Bequeathing hence types of athletic love,
Afternoon this delicious Ninth-month in my forty-
first year,
I proceed for all who are or have been young men,
To tell the secret of my nights and days,
To celebrate the need of comrades.

In such a friendship Whitman saw the balance of sex-passion, which, though it supplies a basis for the clan, cannot provide the wider and more spiritual social bond because of its physical basis. These pages then are of the largest significance. The nobler ranges of that self-expression which is an essential aspect of freedom can only be attained through personal relations with our fellows, and personal relations that are characterized by depth and vitality. For higher human development, friendship must be practised as a fine art. Thus practised it will find a use for those 'magnetic,' those 'electric' fires, the finer energies of the personality, so frequently referred to by Whitman. After we have justified sex, we must mark out its limitations. It is one form of passion, but only one; and the higher life suffers incalculably while we confuse together the different kinds of passion. By the practice of friendship passion clears itself from desire—a thing nowise evil in its own place, but, out of its place, not only mischievous but fatal to development. Thus freed at last, passion may itself become ethereal, and so universal in its scope ; and provide, as the Church well knows, the bond for a true and permanent society, so organically knit together by it as to be worthy the title of Body.

At this period Whitman was curiously attracted by the original Quaker ideals. He sought if he might establish a new "Society of Friends," and "Calamus" contains the outline of his brooding thought and longing. It was to be a pure democracy ; instituted not on the low levels of majority rule, but according to the spiritual needs of the most developed members of the race. As such it would provide the final, unconquerable citadel of freedom. Here are four short poems from this group :

## FAST-ANCHOR'D ETERNAL O LOVE !

Fast-anchor'd eternal O love ! O woman I love !
O bride ! O wife ! more resistless than I can tell, the thought of you !
Then separate, as disembodied or another born,
Ethereal, the last athletic reality, my consolation,
I ascend, I float in the regions of your love O man,
O sharer of my roving life.

## O YOU WHOM I OFTEN AND SILENTLY COME

O you whom I often and silently come where you are that I may be with you,

As I walk by your side or sit near, or remain in
the same room with you,
Little you know the subtle electric fire that for
your sake is playing within me.

## I DREAM'D IN A DREAM

I dream'd in a dream I saw a city invincible to
the attacks of the whole of the rest of the earth,
I dream'd that was the new city of Friends,
Nothing was greater there than the quality of
robust love, it led the rest,
It was seen every hour in the actions of the men
of that city,
And in all their looks and words.

## FOR YOU O DEMOCRACY

Come, I will make the continent indissoluble,
I will make the most splendid race the sun ever
shone upon,
I will make divine magnetic lands,
With the love of comrades,
With the life-long love of comrades.

I will plant companionship thick as trees along
all the rivers of America, and along the shores
of the great lakes, and all over the prairies,
I will make inseparable cities with their arms about
each other's necks,
By the love of comrades,
By the manly love of comrades.

For you these from me, O Democracy, to serve
you ma femme !
For you, for you I am trilling these songs.

"Calamus" shows Whitman prepared for the part he was to play during the now imminent war. His hospital work, with its vast outpourings of devotion, cleansed the air of his soul of its heavy perplexities; and after the storm the shining heights of his thought stood purely outlined against the sky. Much of his perplexity was due to those strange inner experiences, that, amid those days full of colour, made him more aware than others of the regions of life that lie beyond the senses' reach. These experiences naturally enough made him more familiar than other men with the Great Mystery. Death always stood at the side of this singer of life. His 1860 volume closes, like the complete "Leaves of Grass," with poems of departure. In one he spoke of his full rich life:

> The unspeakable love I interchanged with women,
> My joys in the open air—my walks through the Mannahatta,
> The continual goodwill I have met—the curious attachment of young men to me,

and summarizes it all as but a beginning, a first definitive identification of himself. Then, recalling his first promise:

> I remember I said to myself at the winter-close, before my leaves sprang at all, that I would become a candid and unloosed summer-poet

—for thus the line ran at first, referring to the days before his inspiration rose like sap in his soul—he announces the future with the idiomatic cry "So long!"

## SO LONG!

To conclude, I announce what comes after me.

I remember I said before my leaves sprang at all,
I would raise my voice jocund and strong with reference to consummations.

When America does what was promis'd,
When through these States walk a hundred millions of superb persons,
When the rest part away for superb persons and contribute to them,
When breeds of the most perfect mothers denote America,
Then to me and mine our due fruition.

I have press'd through in my own right,
I have sung the body and the soul, war and peace have I sung, and the songs of life and death,
And the songs of birth, and shown that there are many births.

I have offer'd my style to every one, I have journey'd with confident step ;
While my pleasure is yet at the full I whisper *So long !*
And take the young woman's hand and the young man's hand for the last time.

I announce natural persons to arise,
I announce justice triumphant,
I announce uncompromising liberty and equality,
I announce the justification of candour and the justification of pride.

I announce that the identity of these States is a single identity only,

I announce the Union more and more compact,
indissoluble,
I announce splendours and majesties to make all
the previous politics of the earth insignificant.

I announce adhesiveness, I say it shall be limitless,
unloosen'd,
I say you shall yet find the friend you were looking
for.

I announce a man or woman coming, perhaps you
are the one, (*So long !*)
I announce the great individual, fluid as Nature,
chaste, affectionate, compassionate, fully
arm'd.

I announce a life that shall be copious, vehement,
spiritual, bold,
I announce an end that shall lightly and joyfully
meet its translation.

I announce myriads of youths, beautiful, gigantic,
sweet-blooded,
I announce a race of splendid and savage old men.

O thicker and faster—(*So long !*)
O crowding too close upon me,
I foresee too much, it means more than I thought,
It appears to me I am dying.

Hasten throat and sound your last,
Salute me—salute the days once more. Peal the
old cry once more.

Screaming electric, the atmosphere using,
At random glancing, each as I notice absorbing,

Swiftly on, but a little while alighting,
Curious envelop'd messages delivering,
Sparkles hot, seed ethereal down in the dirt dropping,
Myself unknowing, my commission obeying, to question it never daring,
To ages and ages yet the growth of the seed leaving,
To troops out of the war arising, they the tasks I have set promulging,
To women certain whispers of myself bequeathing, their affection me more clearly explaining,
To young men my problems offering—no dallier I—I the muscle of their brains trying,
So I pass, a little time vocal, visible, contrary,
Afterward a melodious echo, passionately bent for, (death making me really undying),
The best of me then when no longer visible, for toward that I have been incessantly preparing.

What is there more, that I lag and pause and crouch extended with unshut mouth?
Is there a single final farewell?

My songs cease, I abandon them,
From behind the screen where I hid I advance personally solely to you.

Camerado, this is no book,
Who touches this touches a man,
(Is it night? are we here together alone?)
It is I you hold and who holds you,
I spring from the pages into your arms—decease calls me forth.

O how your fingers drowse me,
Your breath falls around me like dew, your pulse
    lulls the tympans of my ears,
I feel immerged from head to foot,
Delicious, enough.

Enough O deed impromptu and secret,
Enough O gliding present—enough O summ'd-up
    past.

Dear friend whoever you are take this kiss,
I give it especially to you, do not forget me
I feel like one who has done work for the day to
    retire awhile,
I receive now again of my many translations,
    from my avataras ascending, while others
    doubtless await me,
An unknown sphere more real than I dream'd,
    more direct, darts awakening rays about me,
    *So long !*
Remember my words, I may again return,
I love you, I depart from materials,
I am as one disembodied, triumphant, dead.

## VI

WHILE Whitman was in Boston working on the proofs of his book, Lincoln made his first appearance in New York. An anxious year, a "Year of Meteors," followed. The choice of a Free-soil Republican as President was promptly succeeded by the secession of South Carolina from the Union. Secession became revolt when her guns opened fire on Fort Sumter, April 13, 1861. The North and West responded to Lincoln's call for volunteers; the slave States rallied round South Carolina; while the powerful border States in the vicinity of the capital wavered between the two parties. So began the ruinous conflict, not to be ended, as was everywhere believed, in a short campaign, but to drag out its agony through four cruel years. While Whitman hated war, his soul was in the Union cause and revolted at the idea of schism; yet how much that he passionately loved was in the South we cannot know. His heart was torn by the conflict.

In response to the President's call, George, his younger brother, immediately volunteered. Whitman also, in that hour of supreme national decision, dedicated himself anew to his own high task. I found this note in a manuscript diary at Camden:

> April 16th, 1861.—I have this day, this hour, resolved to inaugurate for myself a pure, perfect, sweet, clean-blooded, robust body, by ignoring all drinks but water and pure milk, and all fat meats, late suppers—a great body, a purged, cleansed, spiritualised, invigorated body.

Remembering Whitman's conception of the relation between body and soul, it is clear that this resolution represents a going into training like that of an athlete before some great event.

In one of the "Calamus" poems he had written:

Earth, my likeness,
Though you look so impassive, ample and spheric
there,
I now suspect that is not all ;
I now suspect there is something fierce in you
eligible to burst forth,
For an athlete is enamour'd of me, and I of him,
But toward him there is something fierce and
terrible in me eligible to burst forth,
I dare not tell it in words, not even in these songs.

Now in "Drum-taps" he finds the answer to this elemental rage within the soul, this thirst for struggle and wrestling.

## RISE O DAYS FROM YOUR FATHOMLESS DEEPS

I

Rise O days from your fathomless deeps, till you
loftier, fiercer sweep,
Long for my soul hungering gymnastic I devour'd
what the earth gave me,
Long I roam'd the woods of the north, long I
watch'd Niagara pouring,
I travel'd the prairies over and slept on their
breast, I cross'd the Nevadas, I cross'd the
plateaus,
I ascended the towering rocks along the Pacific, I
sail'd out to sea,
I sail'd through the storm, I was refresh'd by the
storm,
I watch'd with joy the threatening maws of the
waves,
I mark'd the white combs where they career'd
so high, curling over,

I heard the wind piping, I saw the black clouds,
Saw from below what arose and mounted, (O superb ! O wild as my heart, and powerful !)
Heard the continuous thunder as it bellow'd after the lightning,
Noted the slender and jagged threads of lightning as sudden and fast amid the din they chased each other across the sky ;
These, and such as these, I, elate, saw—saw with wonder, yet pensive and masterful,
All the menacing might of the globe uprisen around me,
Yet there with my soul I fed, I fed content, supercilious.

2

'Twas well, O soul—'twas a good preparation you gave me,
Now we advance our latent and ampler hunger to fill,
Now we go forth to receive what the earth and the sea never gave us,
Not through the mighty woods we go, but through the mightier cities,
Something for us is pouring now more than Niagara pouring,
Torrents of men, (sources and rills of the North-west are you indeed inexhaustible ?)
What, to pavements and homesteads here, what were those storms of the mountains and sea ?
What, to passions I witness around me to-day ? was the sea risen ?
Was the wind piping the pipe of death under the black clouds ?
Lo ! from deeps more unfathomable, something more deadly and savage,

Manhattan rising, advancing with menacing front—Cincinnati, Chicago, unchain'd ;
What was that swell I saw on the ocean ? behold what comes here,
How it climbs with daring feet and hands—how it dashes !
How the true thunder bellows after the lightning —how bright the flashes of lightning !
How Democracy with desperate vengeful port strides on, shown through the dark by those flashes of lightning !
(Yet a mournful wail and low sob I fancied I heard through the dark,
In a lull of the deafening confusion.)

3

Thunder on ! stride on, Democracy ! strike with vengeful stroke !
And do you rise higher than ever yet O days, O cities !
Crash heavier, heavier yet O storms ! you have done me good,
My soul prepared in the mountains absorbs your immortal strong nutriment,
Long had I walk'd my cities, my country roads through farms, only half satisfied,
One doubt nauseous undulating like a snake, crawl'd on the ground before me,
Continually preceding my steps, turning upon me oft, ironically hissing low ;
The cities I loved so well I abandon'd and left, I sped to the certainties suitable to me,
Hungering, hungering, hungering, for primal energies and Nature's dauntlessness,
I refresh'd myself with it only, I could relish it only,

I waited the bursting forth of the pent fire—on the water and air I waited long ;
But now I no longer wait, I am fully satisfied, I am glutted,
I have witness'd the true lightning, I have witness'd my cities electric,
I have lived to behold man burst forth and warlike America rise,
Hence I will seek no more the food of the northern solitary wilds,
No more the mountains roam or sail the stormy sea.

Brooding over great events, Whitman wrote many of his war poems during 1861. Then, in December, finding his brother's name in the lists of the seriously wounded at Fredericksburg, he hurried to the front to nurse him. In the field-hospitals of Virginia he found many New York comrades, with whom, when his brother was able to resume active duty, he journeyed to the capital. Here he became the guest of his Boston friends, Mr. and Mrs. W. D. O'Connor, lingering on in Washington from month to month fulfilling his self-appointed task, as the war continued to pour its human wreckage into the hospital-city. During this time he lived in rigorous simplicity, spending any small surplus he might earn by journalism or beg from his correspondents in the North upon the urgent necessities of the wounded.

Thus, from the beginning of 1862 to the close of the war Whitman's life centres in the Washington hospitals. With the completion of the Boston edition and the writing of his early war poems, his vast vital resources had been set free for a more immediate form of service. In any estimate of his life-work his poems take first place as the expression of a great symbolic personality, one of the possessions of the race for all time. Whatever else he may have done, this was his special contribution. Yet the hospital work, which came as a sort of overplus, a noble by-product of his life, pledges, as nothing else could do, his marriage with the actual American nation in its hour of partial disaster, and so with the whole race. It came to Whitman himself as a needed and sought-for task and discipline. His poems declare that he passionately craved it. Those three years, he afterwards wrote, "aroused and brought out and decided undreamed-of depths of emotion" in him. We can best understand the significance of this chapter of his life from his own words.

In letters to his mother and to the metropolitan papers, he told how, on his first arrival, he felt his utter uselessness; but whenever it came to his leaving the 'youngsters' held on to him convulsively. He convoyed a party of them up to Washington from the front, and began visiting them in their new quarters. The war hospitals differed from those with which he was already acquainted in New York. They offered new and difficult problems to the visitor. But the need for help was overwhelming, and there were few who could give it.

Beginning at first with casual visits . . . to see some of the Brooklyn men, wounded or sick here, I became by degrees more and more drawn in, until I have now been for many weeks quite a devotee to the business, a regular, self-appointed missionary. . . . Almost every day and frequently in the evenings, I visit, in this informal way, one after another of the wards of a hospital. . . . I go around, distributing myself and the contents of my pockets and haversack in infinitesimal quantities, with faith that nearly all of it will, somehow or other, fall on good ground. In many cases, where I find a soldier 'dead broke' and pretty sick, I give half a tumbler of good jelly. I carry a good-sized jar to a ward, have it opened, get a spoon, and taking the head nurse in tow, I go around and distribute it to the most appropriate cases. To others I give an orange or an apple, to others some spiced fruits, to others a small quantity of pickles. Many want tobacco ; I do not encourage any of the boys in its use [he did not use it himself], but where I find they crave it, I supply them. I always carry some, cut up in small plugs, in my pocket. Then I have commissions ; some New York or Connecticut or other soldier will be going home on sick leave, or perhaps discharged, and I must fit him out with good new undershirt, drawers, stockings, etc. But perhaps the greatest welcome is for writing-paper, envelopes, etc. . . .

By these and like means one comes to be better acquainted with individual cases, and so learns everyday peculiar and interesting character, and gets on intimate and soon affectionate terms with noble American young men ; and now is when the real good begins to be done after all. Here, I will egotistically confess, I like to flourish. Even in a medical point of view it is one of the greatest things ; and in a surgical point of view the same. I can testify that friendship has literally cured a fever, and the medicine of daily affection a bad wound. . . .

I shall continue here in Washington for the present, and maybe for the summer, to work as a missionary after my own style, among these hospitals, for I find it in some respects curiously fascinating, with all its sadness. Nor do I find it ended by my doing some good to the sick and dying soldiers. They do me good in return, more than I do them. [*March* 1863.]

Again he wrote :

To many of the wounded and sick, especially the youngsters, there is something in personal love, caresses, and the magnetic flood of sympathy and friendship, that does, in its way, more good than all the medicine in the world. I have spoken of my regular gifts of delicacies, money, tobacco, special articles of food, knick-knacks, etc. etc. But I steadily found, more and more, that I could help, and turn the balance in favour of cure, by the means here alluded to, in a curiously large proportion of cases. The American soldier is full of affection and the yearning for affection. And it comes wonderfully grateful to him to have this yearning gratified when he is laid up with painful wounds or illness, far away from home, among strangers. Many will think this mere sentimentalism, but I know it is the most solid of facts. I believe that even the moving around among the men, or through the ward, of a hearty, healthy, clean, strong, generous-souled person, man or woman, full of humanity and love, sending out invisible constant currents thereof, does immense good to the sick and wounded. [*December* 1864.]

Again :

In these wards or on the field, as I thus continue to go round, I have come to adapt myself to each emergency after its kind or call, however trivial, however solemn ; every one justified and made real under its circumstances—not only visits and cheering talk, and little gifts—not only washing and dressing wounds (I have some cases where the patient is unwilling any one should do this but me)—but passages from the Bible, expounding them, prayer at the bedside, explanations of doctrine, etc. (I think I see my friends smiling at this confession, but I was never more in earnest in my life). In camp and everywhere, I was in the habit of reading and giving recitations to the men. . . .

My habit, when practicable, was to prepare for starting out on one of those daily or nightly tours of from a couple to four or five hours, by fortifying myself with previous rest, the bath, clean clothes, a good meal, and as cheerful an appearance as possible. . . .

Oct. 20th [1863].—To-night, after leaving the hospital at 10 o'clock (I had been on self-imposed duty some five hours, pretty closely confined) I wandered a long time around Washington. The night was sweet, very clear, sufficiently cool, a voluptuous half-moon, slightly golden, the space near it of a transparent blue-gray tinge. . . . The sky, the planets, the constellations all so bright, so calm, so expressively silent, so soothing, after those hospital scenes. I wandered to and fro till the moist moon set, long after midnight. . . .

A great recreation, the past three years, has been in taking long walks out from Washington, five, seven, perhaps ten miles and back ; generally with my friend Pete Doyle, who is as fond of it as I am.

Fine moonlight nights . . . or Sundays—we had these delightful walks, never to be forgotten. [*Dec.* 1865.]

In his hospital work Whitman was spending himself with lavish generosity. His physical health, heightened to a mystical wholeness of being, seemed to endow him with inexhaustible supplies of magnetic power. But what he gave out, with all the burden of personal griefs and anxieties he shouldered, began to sap his strength. In the summer of 1863 he could no longer completely shake off the sense of horror; he began to be haunted by the sights with which he was surrounded. The air in the crowded hospitals became charged, during the heavy heat of a Washington summer, with malarial poisons; and by midsummer 1864 he was really ill ("Spells of deathly faintness, and bad trouble in my head too, and sore throat," "Very bad feeling in my head, fullness and pain," he writes home). He was finally compelled to take a long holiday in and about New York. Back at his post in December, those anxious winter months were doubly anxious for him since his brother was suffering the rigours of imprisonment at Danville. When the long-delayed peace was declared, followed immediately (Good Friday, 1865) by the President's assassination, Whitman was again in Brooklyn. The lilac was in blossom early that year, as no one may now forget for whom his great anthem recalls, better than any other memorial, the nation's mourning and loss.

## WHEN LILACS LAST IN THE DOOR-YARD BLOOM'D

1

When lilacs last in the dooryard bloom'd,
And the great star early droop'd in the western sky in the night,
I mourn'd, and yet shall mourn with ever-returning spring.

Ever-returning spring, trinity sure to me you bring,
Lilac blooming perennial and drooping star in the west,
And thought of him I love.

2

O powerful western fallen star!
O shades of night—O moody, tearful night!
O great star disappear'd—O the black murk that hides the star!
O cruel hands that hold me powerless—O helpless soul of me!
O harsh surrounding cloud that will not free my soul.

3

In the dooryard fronting an old farm-house near the white-wash'd palings,
Stands the lilac-bush tall-growing with heart-shaped leaves of rich green,
With many a pointed blossom rising delicate, with the perfume strong I love,
With every leaf a miracle—and from this bush in the dooryard,
With delicate colour'd blossoms and heart-shaped leaves of rich green,
A sprig with its flower I break.

4

In the swamp in secluded recesses,
A shy and hidden bird is warbling a song.

Solitary the thrush,
The hermit withdrawn to himself, avoiding the settlements,
Sings by himself a song.

Song of the bleeding throat,
Death's outlet song of life, (for well dear brother I know,
If thou wast not granted to sing thou would'st surely die.)

5

Over the breast of the spring, the land, amid cities,
Amid lanes and through old woods, where lately the violets peep'd from the ground, spotting the gray debris,
Amid the grass in the fields each side of the lanes, passing the endless grass,
Passing the yellow-spear'd wheat every grain from its shroud in the dark-brown fields uprisen,
Passing the apple-tree blows of white and pink in the orchards,
Carrying a corpse to where it shall rest in the grave,
Night and day journeys a coffin.

6

Coffin that passes through lanes and streets,
Through day and night with the great cloud darkening the land,
With the pomp of the inloop'd flags with the cities draped in black,

With the show of the States themselves as of
crape-veil'd women standing,
With processions long and winding and the
flambeaus of the night,
With the countless torches lit, with the silent sea
of faces and the unbared heads,
With the waiting depôt, the arriving coffin, and
the sombre faces,
With dirges through the night, with the thousand
voices rising strong and solemn,
With all the mournful voices of the dirges pour'd
around the coffin,
The dim-lit churches and the shuddering organs—
where amid these you journey,
With the tolling tolling bells' perpetual clang,
Here, coffin that slowly passes,
I give you my sprig of lilac.

7

(Nor for you, for one alone,
Blossoms and branches green to coffins all I bring,
For fresh as the morning, thus would I chant a
song for you O sane and sacred death.

All over bouquets of roses,
O death, I cover you over with roses and early lilies,
But mostly and now the lilac that blooms the first,
Copious I break, I break the sprigs from the bushes,
With loaded arms I come, pouring for you,
For you and the coffins all of you O death.)

8

O western orb sailing the heaven,
Now I know what you must have meant as a
month since I walk'd,

As I walk'd in silence the transparent shadowy night,
As I saw you had something to tell as you bent to me night after night,
As you droop'd from the sky low down as if to my side, (while the other stars all look'd on,)
As we wander'd together the solemn night, (for something I know not what kept me from sleep,)
As the night advanced, and I saw on the rim of the west how full you were of woe,
As I stood on the rising ground in the breeze in the cool transparent night,
As I watch'd where you pass'd and was lost in the netherward black of the night,
As my soul in its trouble dissatisfied sank, as where you sad orb,
Concluded, dropt in the night, and was gone.

9

Sing on there in the swamp,
O singer bashful and tender, I hear your notes, I hear your call,
I hear, I come presently, I understand you,
But a moment I linger, for the lustrous star has detain'd me,
The star my departing comrade holds and detains me.

10

O how shall I warble myself for the dead one there I loved?
And how shall I deck my song for the large sweet soul that has gone?
And what shall my perfume be for the grave of him I love?

Sea-winds blown from east and west,
Blown from the Eastern sea and blown from the Western sea, till there on the prairies meeting,
These and with these and the breath of my chant,
I'll perfume the grave of him I love.

11

O what shall I hang on the chamber walls?
And what shall the pictures be that I hang on the walls,
To adorn the burial-house of him I love?

Pictures of growing spring and farms and homes,
With the Fourth-month eve at sundown, and the gray smoke lucid and bright,
With floods of the yellow gold of the gorgeous, indolent, sinking sun, burning, expanding the air,
With the fresh sweet herbage under foot, and the pale green leaves of the trees prolific,
In the distance the flowing glaze, the breast of the river, with a wind-dapple here and there,
With ranging hills on the banks, with many a line against the sky, and shadows,
And the city at hand with dwellings so dense, and stacks of chimneys,
And all the scenes of life and the workshops, and the workmen homeward returning.

12

Lo, body and soul—this land,
My own Manhattan with spires, and the sparkling and hurrying tides, and the ships,
The varied and ample land, the South and the North in the light, Ohio's shores and flashing Missouri,

And ever the far-spreading prairies cover'd with
grass and corn.

Lo, the most excellent sun so calm and haughty,
The violet and purple morn with just-felt breezes,
The gentle soft-born measureless light,
The miracle spreading bathing all, the fulfill'd
noon,
The coming eve delicious, the welcome night and
the stars,
Over my cities shining all, enveloping man and
land.

13

Sing on, sing on you gray-brown bird,
Sing from the swamps, the recesses, pour your
chant from the bushes,
Limitless out of the dusk, out of the cedars and
pines.

Sing on dearest brother, warble your reedy song,
Loud human song, with voice of uttermost woe.

O liquid and free and tender !
O wild and loose to my soul—O wondrous singer !
You only I hear—yet the star holds me, (but will
soon depart,)
Yet the lilac with mastering odour holds me.

14

Now while I sat in the day and look'd forth,
In the close of the day with its light and the fields
of spring, and the farmers preparing their
crops,
In the large unconscious scenery of my land with
its lakes and forests,
In the heavenly aerial beauty, (after the perturb'd
winds and the storms,)

Under the arching heavens of the afternoon swift
passing, and the voices of children and
women,
The many-moving sea-tides, and I saw the ships
how they sail'd,
And the summer approaching with richness, and
the fields all busy with labour,
And the infinite separate houses, how they all
went on, each with its meals and minutia of
daily usages,
And the streets how their throbbings throbb'd,
and the cities pent—lo, then and there,
Falling upon them all and among them all,
enveloping me with the rest,
Appear'd the cloud, appear'd the long black trail,
And I knew death, its thought, and the sacred
knowledge of death.

Then with the knowledge of death as walking one
side of me,
And the thought of death close-walking the other
side of me,
And I in the middle as with companions, and as
holding the hands of companions,
I fled forth to the hiding receiving night that talks
not,
Down to the shores of the water, the path by the
swamp in the dimness,
To the solemn shadowy cedars and ghostly pines
so still.

And the singer so shy to the rest receiv'd me,
The gray-brown bird I know receiv'd us comrades
three,
And he sang the carol of death, and a verse for
him I love.

From deep secluded recesses,
From the fragrant cedars and the ghostly pines so still,
Came the carol of the bird.

And the charm of the carol rapt me,
As I held as if by their hands my comrades in the night,
And the voice of my spirit tallied the song of the bird.

*Come lovely and soothing death,*
*Undulate round the world, serenely arriving, arriving,*
*In the day, in the night, to all, to each,*
*Sooner or later delicate death.*

*Prais'd be the fathomless universe,*
*For life and joy, and for objects and knowledge curious,*
*And for love, sweet love—but praise! praise! praise!*
*For the sure-enwinding arms of cool-enfolding death.*

*Dark mother always gliding near with soft feet,*
*Have none chanted for thee a chant of fullest welcome?*
*Then I chant it for thee, I glorify thee above all,*
*I bring thee a song that when thou must indeed come, come unfalteringly.*

*Approach strong deliveress,*
*When it is so, when thou hast taken them I joyously sing the dead,*
*Lost in the loving floating ocean of thee,*
*Laved in the flood of thy bliss O death.*

*From me to thee glad serenades,*
*Dances for thee I propose saluting thee, adornments and feastings for thee,*
*And the sights of the open landscape and the high-spread sky are fitting,*
*And life and the fields, and the huge and thoughtful night.*

*The night in silence under many a star,*
*The ocean shore and the husky whispering wave whose voice I know,*
*And the soul turning to thee O vast and well-veil'd death,*
*And the body gratefully nestling close to thee.*

*Over the tree-tops I float thee a song,*
*Over the rising and sinking waves, over the myriad fields and the prairies wide,*
*Over the dense-pack'd cities all and the teeming wharves and ways,*
*I float this carol with joy, with joy to thee O death.*

15

To the tally of my soul,
Loud and strong kept up the gray-brown bird,
With pure deliberate notes spreading filling the night.

Loud in the pines and cedars dim,
Clear in the freshness moist and the swamp-perfume,
And I with my comrades there in the night.

While my sight that was bound in my eyes unclosed,
As to long panoramas of visions.

And I saw askant the armies,
I saw as in noiseless dreams hundreds of battle-flags,
Borne through the smoke of the battles and pierc'd with missiles I saw them,
And carried hither and yon through the smoke, and torn and bloody,
And at last but a few shreds left on the staffs, (and all in silence,)
And the staffs all splinter'd and broken.

I saw battle-corpses, myriads of them,
And the white skeletons of young men, I saw them,
I saw the debris and debris of all the slain soldiers of the war,
But I saw they were not as was thought,
They themselves were fully at rest, they suffer'd not,
The living remain'd and suffer'd, the mother suffer'd,
And the wife and the child and the musing comrade suffer'd,
And the armies that remain'd suffer'd.

16

Passing the visions, passing the night,
Passing, unloosing the hold of my comrades' hands,
Passing the song of the hermit bird and the tallying song of my soul,
Victorious song, death's outlet song, yet varying ever-altering song,
As low and wailing, yet clear the notes, rising and falling, flooding the night,

Sadly sinking and fainting, as warning and warning, and yet again bursting with joy,
Covering the earth and filling the spread of the heaven,
As that powerful psalm in the night I heard from recesses,
Passing, I leave thee lilac with heart-shaped leaves,
I leave thee there in the door-yard, blooming, returning with spring.

I cease from my song for thee,
From my gaze on thee in the west, fronting the west, communing with thee,
O comrade lustrous with silver face in the night.

Yet each to keep and all, retrievements out of the night,
The song, the wondrous chant of the gray-brown bird,
And the tallying chant, the echo arous'd in my soul,
With the lustrous and drooping star with the countenance full of woe,
With the holders holding my hand nearing the call of the bird,
Comrades mine and I in the midst, and their memory ever to keep, for the dead I loved so well,
For the sweetest, wisest soul of all my days and lands—and this for his dear sake,
Lilac and star and bird twined with the chant of my soul,
There in the fragrant pines and the cedars dusk and dim.

The poem has close affinity with "Out of the Cradle." Here it is not the moon but the evening star that shines through the dusk ; the bird is the swamp-frequenting hermit-thrush, instead of the mocking-bird, "the visitor from Alabama" among the seashore briars. But it is lilac-time in each nocturne ; and each is a chant of bereavement, a recitative and aria—the bird's song—with the refrain, expressed or implicit in each, of "death, death, death, death, death." Written between 1859 and 1865, these two poems represent Whitman's most melodious achievements, the most perfect examples of his genius viewed from the literary side. They are not, perhaps, so charged with creative force as some of the work of the preceding five years, but the potency behind them is felt through the transparent beauty, the serene universality of their utterance.

The Lincoln anthem, written after the main body of "Drum-taps," was added to that collection when it was published in 1865–6. From "Drum-taps" I may quote two curiously metrical poems fitted to the marching of drums.

### ETHIOPIA SALUTING THE COLOURS

Who are you dusky woman, so ancient hardly
human,
With your woolly-white and turban'd head, and
bare bony feet ?
Why rising by the roadside here, do you the
colours greet ?

('Tis while our army lines Carolina's sands and
pines,

Forth from thy hovel door thou Ethiopia com'st
to me,
As under doughty Sherman I march toward the
sea.)

*Me master years a hundred since from my parents
sunder'd,*
*A little child, they caught me as the savage beast is
caught,*
*Then hither me across the sea the cruel slaver
brought.*

No further does she say, but lingering all the day,
Her high-borne turban'd head she wags, and rolls
her darkling eye,
And courtesies to the regiments, the guidons
moving by.

What is it fateful woman, so blear, hardly human ?
Why wag your head with turban bound, yellow,
red and green ?
Are the things so strange and marvellous you see
or have seen ?

## DIRGE FOR TWO VETERANS

The last sunbeam
Lightly falls from the finish'd Sabbath,
On the pavement here, and there beyond it is
looking
Down a new-made double grave.

Lo, the moon ascending,
Up from the east the silvery round moon,
Beautiful over the house-tops, ghastly, phantom
moon,
Immense and silent moon.

I see a sad procession,
And I hear the sound of coming full-key'd bugles,
All the channels of the city streets they're flooding,
As with voices and with tears.

I hear the great drums pounding,
And the small drums steady whirring,
And every blow of the great convulsive drums,
Strikes me through and through.

For the son is brought with the father,
(In the foremost ranks of the fierce assault they fell,
Two veterans son and father dropt together,
And the double grave awaits them.)

Now nearer blow the bugles,
And the drums strike more convulsive,
And the daylight o'er the pavement quite has faded,
And the strong dead-march enwraps me.

In the eastern sky up-buoying,
The sorrowful vast phantom moves illumin'd,
('Tis some mother's large transparent face,
In heaven brighter growing.)

O strong dead-march you please me !
O moon immense with your silvery face you soothe me !
O my soldiers twain ! O my veterans passing to burial !
What I have I also give you.

The moon gives you light,
And the bugles and the drums give you music,
And my heart, O my soldiers, my veterans,
My heart gives you love.

I need hardly say that during these hospital years Whitman knew and felt to the full the awful moral and physical cost of war. Indeed I think his quarrel with his intimate friend O'Connor, the fiery Abolitionist, turned partly upon this. For Whitman sometimes felt that the whole negro race was not worth the price at which America was purchasing emancipation. Unquestionably, something of America herself, some unfulfilled promise of those earlier years, corresponding to the promise Wordsworth in his youth had recognized hovering in the blissful air of new-awakened France, perished forever in that deadly struggle. Whitman has given us a suggestion of this prophetic season that immediately preceded the war in the later lines of a poem written, I think, about 1861 :

### YEARS OF THE MODERN !

Years of the modern ! years of the unperform'd !
Your horizon rises, I see it parting away for more
 august dramas,
I see not America only, not only Liberty's nation
 but other nations preparing,
I see tremendous entrances and exits, new com-
 binations, the solidarity of races,
I see that force advancing with irresistible power
 on the world's stage,
(Have the old forces, the old wars, played their
 parts ? are the acts suitable to them closed ?)
I see Freedom, completely arm'd and victorious
 and very haughty, with Law on one side and
 Peace on the other,

A stupendous trio all issuing forth against the idea of caste ;
What historic denouements are these we so rapidly approach ?
I see men marching and countermarching by swift millions,
I see the frontiers and boundaries of the old aristocracies broken,
I see the landmarks of European kings removed,
I see this day the People beginning their landmarks, (all others give way ;)
Never were such sharp questions ask'd as this day,
Never was average man, his soul, more energetic, more like a God,
Lo, how he urges and urges, leaving the masses no rest !
His daring foot is on land and sea everywhere, he colonizes the Pacific, the archipelagoes,
With the steamship, the electric telegraph, the newspaper, the wholesale engines of war,
With these and the world-spreading factories he interlinks all geography, all lands ;
What whispers are these O lands, running ahead of you, passing under the seas ?
Are all nations communing ? is there going to be but one heart to the globe ?
Is humanity forming en-masse ? for lo, tyrants tremble, crowns grow dim,
The earth, restive, confronts a new era, perhaps a general divine war,
No one knows what will happen next, such portents fill the days and nights ;
Years prophetical ! the space ahead as I walk, as I vainly try to pierce it, is full of phantoms,

Unborn deeds, things soon to be, project their
shapes around me,
This incredible rush and heat, this strange ecstatic
fever of dreams, O years!
Your dreams O years, how they penetrate through
me! (I know not whether I sleep or wake;)
The perform'd America and Europe grow dim,
retiring in shadow behind me,
The unperform'd, more gigantic than ever, advance, advance upon me.

Whitman had hated war; yet he accepted its tragic cost. Blindness of heart had created its necessity; it need never have been. Hating and accepting it, he sang of it as few have ever sung. He had himself no fear of death, nor did he ever count it too high a price to pay for freedom; but the stubborn question persists: Does war ever bring any nearer the freedom for which he stood? Perhaps that was not then the question. To him, as to America, the cause of the Union, once it was assailed, seemed the last stronghold of political liberty that must be preserved at any cost.

Three more brief poems from "Drum-taps," sounding perhaps a truer note than that of exultation, may here be added:

## YEAR THAT TREMBLED AND REEL'D BENEATH ME

Year that trembled and reel'd beneath me!
Your summer wind was warm enough, yet the
air I breathed froze me,

A thick gloom fell through the sunshine and
darken'd me,
Must I change my triumphant songs ? said I to
myself,
Must I indeed learn to chant the cold dirges of the
baffled ?
And sullen hymns of defeat ?

## NOT THE PILOT

Not the pilot has charged himself to bring his
ship into port, though beaten back and many
times baffled ;
Not the pathfinder penetrating inland weary and
long,
By deserts parch'd, snows chill'd, rivers wet,
perseveres till he reaches his destination,
More than I have charged myself, heeded or un-
heeded, to compose a march for these States,
For a battle-call, rousing to arms if need be,
years, centuries hence.

## RECONCILIATION

Word over all, beautiful as the sky,
Beautiful that war and all its deeds of carnage
must in time be utterly lost,
That the hands of the sisters Death and Night
incessantly softly wash again, and ever again,
this soil'd world ;
For my enemy is dead, a man divine as myself is
dead,
I look where he lies white-faced and still in the
coffin—I draw near,
Bend down and touch lightly with my lips the
white face in the coffin.

# WHITMAN & HIS POETRY

## VII

AFTER many a fruitless effort, Whitman had obtained a clerkship in the Department of the Interior ; but within a few months (at midsummer 1865) his 'services were dispensed with.' His chief had been surreptitiously reading a copy of "Leaves of Grass," extracted from his desk. The undeclared but widely known ground of this dismissal evoked O'Connor's fiery defence, "The Good Gray Poet." Whitman did not suffer. He was given a similar post, worth about £300, under his friend Mr. Hubley Ashton in another Government department, and retained it for the next nine years—years of comparative affluence.

The hospital visits continued for a time after the declaration of peace, but with the end of the war the great strain was over. It must not, of course, be imagined that Whitman had spent the preceding three years wholly in the wards. Apart from the necessity of earning a living, which he had only accomplished with difficulty, he had continued his rôle as spectator of events. When the war was over, and his hale friends began to outnumber the crippled, his long night walks became jolly social excursions, in many of which Mr. John Burroughs shared. He was one of that group of devoted friends who now surrounded the poet, an ideal society of able, thoughtful, and enthusiastic young married men in whose homes he was always more than welcome. The influence both of decreased physical vitality and of increased intercourse with such men and women is reflected in the less aggressive, more restrained tone of his work. As some one has said, there was no ground for censorship in any of the poems written after 1860. A new phase of his life had then begun. Naturally its distinguishing note was that of American nationality; and his "Democratic Vistas," the remarkable and eloquent tractate in which he replies to Carlyle's "Shooting Niagara," is dedicated to this theme. While it ruthlessly exposes the cheap current complacency of Americans, it is a declaration of ultimate faith in America herself. Whitman beheld the Republic standing forth perilously, a challenge to every enemy of freedom. Were she not maintained by a higher practice of republican virtues than had yet been known, she must fall beneath their covert attacks. Like the prophets of Israel, while denouncing her failings and paltry ideal of success, he proclaims the divine rôle of his nation. He sees in her government the means of fostering a wholly free, soul-conscious, passionate race, that shall become the mother of free nations.

Recent years had brought Whitman wider recognition both at home and abroad. In England he was hailed about this time as the poet of freedom by such men as Swinburne and the Rossettis, J. A. Symonds, F. W. H. Myers, and Ed. Dowden; while Björnson, Rudolf Schmidt, and Freiligrath were among his Continental admirers. In 1868 W. M. Rossetti published a selection from " Leaves of Grass " comprising more than a hundred of the poems, together with the first preface, which naturally appealed to the founders of " The Germ." Certain poems were excluded, among others the " Song of Myself," but none of those given suffered any kind of mutilation.

Western as he essentially was, Whitman's mystical tone and the emphasis he laid on physical health as the essential basis for further personal development often seem to relate him to the Eastern rather than to the Western mystics. This relation is emphasized in his " Passage to India," the most important poem of this period. It was suggested by two events of 1869, the completion of the Suez Canal and of the Pacific Railway. In " Passage to India," he once declared, there is " more of the essential ultimate me " than in any other poem.

## PASSAGE TO INDIA

I

Singing my days,
Singing the great achievements of the present,
Singing the strong light works of engineers,
Our modern wonders, (the antique ponderous Seven
  outvied,)
In the Old World the east the Suez canal,
The New by its mighty railroad spann'd,
The seas inlaid with eloquent gentle wires ;
Yet first to sound, and ever sound, the cry with
  thee O soul,
The Past ! the Past ! the Past !

The Past—the dark unfathom'd retrospect !
The teeming gulf—the sleepers and the shadows !
The past—the infinite greatness of the past !
For what is the present after all but a growth out of the past ?
(As a projectile form'd, impell'd, passing a certain line, still keeps on,
So the present, utterly form'd, impell'd by the past.)

2

Passage O soul to India !
Eclaircise the myths Asiatic, the primitive fables.

Not you alone proud truths of the world,
Nor you alone ye facts of modern science,
But myths and fables of eld, Asia's, Africa's fables,
The far-darting beams of the spirit, the unloos'd dreams,
The deep diving bibles and legends,
The daring plots of the poets, the elder religions ;
O you temples fairer than lilies pour'd over by the rising sun !
O you fables spurning the known, eluding the hold of the known, mounting to heaven !
You lofty and dazzling towers, pinnacled, red as roses, burnish'd with gold !
Towers of fables immortal fashion'd from mortal dreams !
You too I welcome and fully the same as the rest !
You too with joy I sing.

Passage to India !
Lo, soul, seest thou not God's purpose from the first ?
The earth to be spann'd, connected by network,

The races, neighbours, to marry and be given in
 marriage,
The oceans to be cross'd, the distant brought near,
The lands to be welded together.

A worship new I sing,
You captains, voyagers, explorers, yours,
You engineers, you architects, machinists, yours,
You, not for trade or transportation only,
But in God's name, and for thy sake O soul.

3

Passage to India !
Lo soul for thee of tableaus twain,
I see in one the Suez canal initiated, open'd,
I see the procession of steamships, the Empress
 Eugenie's leading the van,
I mark from on deck the strange landscape, the
 pure sky, the level sand in the distance,
I pass swiftly the picturesque groups, the workmen
 gather'd,
The gigantic dredging machines.

In one again, different, (yet thine, all thine, O soul,
 the same,)
I see over my own continent the Pacific railroad
 surmounting every barrier,
I see continual trains of cars winding along the
 Platte carrying freight and passengers,
I hear the locomotives rushing and roaring, and
 the shrill steam-whistle,
I hear the echoes reverberate through the grandest
 scenery in the world,
I cross the Laramie plains, I note the rocks in
 grotesque shapes, the buttes,
I see the plentiful larkspur and wild onions, the
 barren, colourless, sage-deserts,

I see in glimpses afar or towering immediately
above me the great mountains, I see the Wind
river and the Wahsatch mountains,
I see the Monument mountain and the Eagle's
Nest, I pass the Promontory, I ascend the
Nevadas,
I scan the noble Elk mountain and wind around
its base,
I see the Humboldt range, I thread the valley and
cross the river,
I see the clear waters of lake Tahoe, I see forests
of majestic pines,
Or crossing the great desert, the alkaline plains, I
behold enchanting mirages of waters and
meadows,
Marking through these and after all, in duplicate
slender lines,
Bridging the three or four thousand miles of land
travel,
Tying the Eastern to the Western sea,
The road between Europe and Asia.

(Ah Genoese thy dream ! thy dream !
Centuries after thou art laid in thy grave,
The shore thou foundest verifies thy dream.)

4

Passage to India !
Struggles of many a captain, tales of many a
sailor dead,
Over my mood stealing and spreading they come,
Like clouds and cloudlets in the unreach'd sky.

Along all history, down the slopes,
As a rivulet running, sinking now, and now again
to the surface rising,

A ceaseless thought, a varied train—lo, soul, to
thee, thy sight, they rise,
The plans, the voyages again, the expeditions ;
Again Vasco de Gama sails forth,
Again the knowledge gain'd, the mariner's compass,
Lands found and nations born, thou born America,
For purpose vast, man's long probation fill'd,
Thou rondure of the world at last accomplish'd.

5

O vast Rondure, swimming in space,
Cover'd all over with visible power and beauty,
Alternate light and day and the teeming spiritual darkness,
Unspeakable high processions of sun and moon and countless stars above,
Below, the manifold grass and waters, animals, mountains, trees,
With inscrutable purpose, some hidden prophetic intention,
Now first it seems my thought begins to span thee.

Down from the gardens of Asia descending radiating,
Adam and Eve appear, then their myriad progeny after them,
Wandering, yearning, curious, with restless explorations,
With questionings, baffled, formless, feverish, with never-happy hearts,
With that sad incessant refrain, *Wherefore unsatisfied soul ?* and *Whither O mocking life ?*

Ah who shall soothe these feverish children ?
Who justify these restless explorations ?

Who speak the secret of impassive earth?
Who bind it to us? what is this separate Nature
so unnatural?
What is this earth to our affections? (unloving
earth, without a throb to answer ours,
Cold earth, the place of graves.)

Yet soul be sure the first intent remains, and shall
be carried out,
Perhaps even now the time has arrived.

After the seas are all cross'd, (as they seem already
cross'd,)
After the great captains and engineers have
accomplish'd their work,
After the noble inventors, after the scientists, the
chemist, the geologist, ethnologist,
Finally shall come the poet worthy that name,
The true son of God shall come singing his songs.

Then not your deeds only O voyagers, O scientists
and inventors, shall be justified,
All these hearts as of fretted children shall be
sooth'd,
All affection shall be fully responded to, the secret
shall be told,
All these separations and gaps shall be taken up
and hook'd and link'd together,
The whole earth, this cold, impassive, voiceless
earth, shall be completely justified,
Trinitas divine shall be gloriously accomplish'd
and compacted by the true son of God, the
poet,
(He shall indeed pass the straits and conquer the
mountains,
He shall double the cape of Good Hope to some
purpose,)

Nature and Man shall be disjoin'd and diffused
no more,
The true son of God shall absolutely fuse them.

6

Year at whose wide-flung door I sing!
Year of the purpose accomplish'd!
Year of the marriage of continents, climates and
oceans!
(No mere doge of Venice now wedding the
Adriatic,)
I see O year in you the vast terraqueous globe
given and giving all,
Europe to Asia, Africa join'd, and they to the
New World,
The lands, geographies, dancing before you, holding
a festival garland,
As brides and bridegrooms hand in hand.

Passage to India!
Cooling airs from Caucasus far, soothing cradle
of man,
The river Euphrates flowing, the past lit up again.

Lo soul, the retrospect brought forward,
The old, most populous, wealthiest of earth's lands,
The streams of the Indus and the Ganges and
their many affluents,
(I my shores of America walking to-day behold,
resuming all,)
The tale of Alexander on his warlike marches
suddenly dying,
On one side China and on the other side Persia
and Arabia,
To the south the great seas and the bay of Bengal,
The flowing literatures, tremendous epics, religions
castes,

Old occult Brahma interminably far back, the
tender and junior Buddha,
Central and southern empires and all their belongings, possessors,
The wars of Tamerlane, the reign of Aurungzebe,
The traders, rulers, explorers, Moslems, Venetians,
Byzantium, the Arabs, Portuguese,
The first travellers famous yet, Marco Polo,
Batouta the Moor,
Doubts to be solv'd, the map incognita, blanks to
be fill'd,
The foot of man unstay'd, the hands never at rest,
Thyself O soul that will not brook a challenge.

The mediæval navigators rise before me,
The world of 1492, with its awaken'd enterprise,
Something swelling in humanity now like the sap
of the earth in spring,
The sunset splendour of chivalry declining.

And who art thou sad shade?
Gigantic, visionary, thyself a visionary,
With majestic limbs and pious beaming eyes,
Spreading around with every look of thine a golden
world,
Enhuing it with gorgeous hues.

As the chief histrion,
Down the footlights walks in some great scena,
Dominating the rest I see the Admiral himself,
(History's type of courage, action, faith,)
Behold him sail from Palos leading his little fleet,
His voyage behold, his return, his great fame,
His misfortunes, calumniators, behold him a
prisoner, chain'd,
Behold his dejection, poverty, death.

(Curious in time I stand, noting the efforts of
 heroes,
Is the deferment long? bitter the slander, poverty,
 death?
Lies the seed unreck'd for centuries in the ground?
 lo, to God's due occasion,
Uprising in the night, it sprouts, blooms,
And fills the earth with use and beauty.)

7

Passage indeed O soul to primal thought,
Not lands and seas alone, thy own clear freshness,
The young maturity of brood and bloom,
To realms of budding bibles.

O soul, repressless, I with thee and thou with me,
Thy circumnavigation of the world begin,
Of man, the voyage of his mind's return,
To reason's early paradise,
Back, back to wisdom's birth, to innocent intui-
 tions,
Again with fair creation.

8

O we can wait no longer,
We too take ship O soul,
Joyous we too launch out on trackless seas,
Fearless for unknown shores on waves of ecstasy
 to sail,
Amid the wafting winds, (thou pressing me to
 thee, I thee to me, O soul,)
Carolling free, singing our song of God,
Chanting our chant of pleasant exploration.

With laugh and many a kiss,
(Let others deprecate, let others weep for sin,
 remorse, humiliation,)

O soul thou pleasest me, I thee.

Ah more than any priest O soul we too believe in God,
But with the mystery of God we dare not dally.

O soul thou pleasest me, I thee,
Sailing these seas or on the hills, or waking in the night,
Thoughts, silent thoughts, of Time and Space and Death, like waters flowing,
Bear me indeed as through the regions infinite,
Whose air I breathe, whose ripples hear, lave me all over,
Bathe me O God in thee, mounting to thee,
I and my soul to range in range of thee.

O Thou transcendent,
Nameless, the fibre and the breath,
Light of the light, shedding forth universes, thou centre of them,
Thou mightier centre of the true, the good, the loving,
Thou moral, spiritual fountain—affection's source—thou reservoir,
(O pensive soul of me—O thirst unsatisfied—waitest not there ?
Waitest not haply for us somewhere there the Comrade perfect ?)
Thou pulse—thou motive of the stars, suns, systems,
That, circling, move in order, safe, harmonious,
Athwart the shapeless vastnesses of space,
How should I think, how breathe a single breath, how speak, if, out of myself,
I could not launch, to those, superior universes ?

Swiftly I shrivel at the thought of God,
At Nature and its wonders, Time and Space and Death,
But that I, turning, call to thee O soul, thou actual Me,
And lo, thou gently masterest the orbs,
Thou matest Time, smilest content at Death,
And fillest, swellest full the vastnesses of Space.

Greater than stars or suns,
Bounding O soul thou journeyest forth ;
What love than thine and ours could wider amplify ?
What aspirations, wishes, outvie thine and ours O soul ?
What dreams of the ideal ? what plans of purity, perfection, strength ?
What cheerful willingness for others' sake to give up all ?
For others' sake to suffer all ?

Reckoning ahead O soul, when thou, the time achiev'd,
The seas all cross'd, weather'd the capes, the voyage done,
Surrounded, copest, frontest God, yieldest, the aim attain'd,
As fill'd with friendship, love complete, the Elder Brother found,
The Younger melts in fondness in his arms.

9

Passage to more than India !
Are thy wings plumed indeed for such far flights ?
O soul, voyagest thou indeed on voyages like those ?
Disportest thou on waters such as those ?

Soundest below the Sanscrit and the Vedas ?
Then have thy bent unleash'd.

Passage to you, your shores, ye aged fierce enigmas !
Passage to you, to mastership of you, ye strangling problems !
You, strew'd with the wrecks of skeletons, that, living, never reach'd you.

Passage to more than India !
O secret of the earth and sky !
Of you O waters of the sea ! O winding creeks and rivers !
Of you O woods and fields ! of you strong mountains of my land !
Of you O prairies ! of you gray rocks !
O morning red ! O clouds ! O rain and snows !
O day and night, passage to you !

O sun and moon and all you stars ! Sirius and Jupiter !
Passage to you !

Passage, immediate passage ! the blood burns in my veins !
Away O soul ! hoist instantly the anchor !
Cut the hawsers—haul out—shake out every sail !
Have we not stood here like trees in the ground long enough ?
Have we not grovell'd here long enough, eating and drinking like mere brutes ?
Have we not darken'd and dazed ourselves with books long enough ?

Sail forth—steer for the deep waters only,
Reckless O soul, exploring, I with thee, and thou with me,

For we are bound where mariner has not yet
    dared to go,
And we will risk the ship, ourselves and all.

O my brave soul!
O farther farther sail!
O daring joy, but safe! are they not all the seas
    of God?
O farther, farther, farther sail!

Besides "Passage to India," the long Washington sojourn, with its uncomfortable boarding-house background, produced but few poems of foremost rank after "President Lincoln's Burial Hymn." They are generally characterized by more formal and philosophical treatment and are less instinct with inspiration than "Drum-taps" and his earlier work. Some of the brief songs of death, especially "Joy, Shipmate, Joy!" "Now Finalè to the Shore," "Darest thou now, O Soul!" are among the most beautiful of his lyrics, while "The City Dead-house" and "To thee, Old Cause" still ring with the old power. "The Mystic Trumpeter" also belongs to these years. But I can find little fresh inspiration in such pages as the "Song of the Exposition" or "Thou Mother with thy Equal Brood," poems written to be read on specific occasions. They contain fine sonorous lines, but lack inevitableness. Even the "Song of the Universal," deservedly a favourite, is in strangest contrast with his early work. Here are "the stock poetic touches" so carefully omitted then; phrases which often, at this time, destroy the direct reality of his work. For example, in 1867 he actually prefaced the noble early lines of "The Answerer" with the phrase "Now list to my morning's romanza," in the worst operatic style. Indeed, Whitman recognized, rather sadly, this falling off in the urgency of his inspiration; for in 1872, in the preface to "Thou Mother with thy Equal Brood," he questioned whether poetry had not become a habit to him, with "no real need of saying anything further."

Whitman had been ten years in Washington, and was nearly fifty-four, when the more and more frequently recurring spells of head trouble culminated in a slight paralytic seizure. This disaster to his health was no more due to dissipation, as some ignorant critics have suggested, than is the phthisis and nervous breakdown which fills the Riviera and the Engadine with wrecked social and intellectual workers. Every intelligent observer sees that overstrain lies in wait for none more relentlessly than for the sensitive and conscientious, the generous and heroic. It punishes the natural laws infringed by these—wrongly infringed we may admit, but not ignobly.

Whitman was gradually beginning to take up work again when his old mother, who had left Brooklyn to live with her soldier son near Philadelphia, fell seriously ill. He hurried to her, and was with her when she died. Her death was for him Fate's heaviest blow. She had always been the centre of his individual life, and with her loss he felt himself a homeless man. The passionate love of his heart had centred above all in two objects, his soldier-charges and his mother. Now he lay stranded in Camden, having lost them both, and the whole circle of his friends into the bargain. For the next three years he remained, only half alive, a prisoner under the roof of his kindly but uncongenial brother. To this period belong the "Songs" of "the Universal" and of "the Redwood Tree," and the "Prayer of Columbus," an autobiographical fragment written under darkest skies.

## PRAYER OF COLUMBUS

A batter'd, wreck'd old man,
Thrown on this savage shore, far, far from home,
Pent by the sea and dark rebellious brows, twelve dreary months,
Sore, stiff with many toils, sicken'd and nigh to death,
I take my way along the island's edge,
Venting a heavy heart.

I am too full of woe !
Haply I may not live another day ;
I cannot rest O God, I cannot eat or drink or sleep,
Till I put forth myself, my prayer, once more to Thee,
Breathe, bathe myself once more in Thee, commune with Thee,
Report myself once more to Thee.

Thou knowest my years entire, my life,
My long and crowded life of active work, not adoration merely ;

Thou knowest the prayers and vigils of my youth,
Thou knowest my manhood's solemn and visionary meditations,
Thou knowest how before I commenced I devoted all to come to Thee,
Thou knowest I have in age ratified all those vows and strictly kept them,
Thou knowest I have not once lost nor faith nor ecstasy in Thee,
In shackles, prison'd, in disgrace, repining not,
Accepting all from Thee, as duly come from Thee.

All my emprises have been fill'd with Thee,
My speculations, plans, begun and carried on in thoughts of Thee,
Sailing the deep or journeying the land for Thee ;
Intentions, purports, aspirations mine, leaving results to Thee.

O I am sure they really came from Thee,
The urge, the ardour, the unconquerable will,
The potent, felt, interior command, stronger than words,
A message from the Heavens whispering to me even in sleep,
These sped me on.

By me and these the work so far accomplish'd,
By me earth's elder cloy'd and stifled lands uncloy'd, unloos'd,
By me the hemispheres rounded and tied, the unknown to the known.

The end I know not, it is all in Thee,
Or small or great I know not—haply what broad fields, what lands,

Haply the brutish measureless human undergrowth I know,
Transplanted there may rise to stature, knowledge worthy Thee,
Haply the swords I know may there indeed be turn'd to reaping-tools,
Haply the lifeless cross I know, Europe's dead cross, may bud and blossom there.

One effort more, my altar this bleak sand ;
That Thou O God my life hast lighted,
With ray of light, steady, ineffable, vouchsafed of Thee,
Light rare untellable, lighting the very light,
Beyond all signs, descriptions, languages ;
For that O God, be it my latest word, here on my knees,
Old, poor, and paralyzed, I thank Thee.

My terminus near,
The clouds already closing in upon me,
The voyage balk'd, the course disputed, lost,
I yield my ships to Thee.

My hands, my limbs grow nerveless,
My brain feels rack'd, bewilder'd,
Let the old timbers part, I will not part,
I will cling fast to Thee, O God, though the waves buffet me,
Thee, Thee at least I know.

Is it the prophet's thought I speak, or am I raving ?
What do I know of life ? what of myself ?
I know not even my own work past or present,
Dim ever-shifting guesses of it spread before me,
Of newer better worlds, their mighty parturition,
Mocking, perplexing me.

And these things I see suddenly, what mean they ?
As if some miracle, some hand divine unseal'd
my eyes,
Shadowy vast shapes smile through the air and
sky,
And on the distant waves sail countless ships,
And anthems in new tongues I hear saluting me.

Partly for its own sake, partly as a contrast with the earlier poems quoted on previous pages, I give here the "Song of the Universal," with its tendency to the iambic structure, its accumulation of abstract rather than concrete images, and withal its undeniable Whitman flavour and authenticity.

## SONG OF THE UNIVERSAL

1

Come said the Muse,
Sing me a song no poet yet has chanted,
Sing me the universal.

In this broad earth of ours,
Amid the measureless grossness and the slag,
Enclosed and safe within its central heart,
Nestles the seed perfection.

By every life a share or more or less,
None born but it is born, conceal'd or unconceal'd
the seed is waiting.

2

Lo ! keen-eyed towering science,
As from tall peaks the modern overlooking,
Successive absolute fiats issuing.

Yet again, lo ! the soul, above all science,
For it has history gather'd like husks around the globe,
For it the entire star-myriads roll through the sky.

In spiral routes by long detours,
(As a much-tacking ship upon the sea,)
For it the partial to the permanent flowing,
For it the real to the ideal tends.

For it the mystic evolution,
Not the right only justified, what we call evil also justified.

Forth from their masks, no matter what,
From the huge festering trunk, from craft and guile and tears,
Health to emerge and joy, joy universal.

Out of the bulk, the morbid and the shallow,
Out of the bad majority, the varied countless frauds of men and states,
Electric, antiseptic yet, cleaving, suffusing all,
Only the good is universal.

3

Over the mountain-growths disease and sorrow,
An uncaught bird is ever hovering, hovering,
High in the purer, happier air.

From imperfection's murkiest cloud,
Darts always forth one ray of perfect light,
One flash of heaven's glory.

To fashion's, custom's discord,
To the mad Babel-din, the deafening orgies,
Soothing each lull a strain is heard, just heard,
From some far shore the final chorus sounding.

O the blest eyes, the happy hearts,
That see, that know the guiding thread so fine,
Along the mighty labyrinth.

4

And thou America,
For the scheme's culmination, its thought and its
    reality,
For these (not for thyself) thou hast arrived.

Thou too surroundest all,
Embracing carrying welcoming all, thou too by
    pathways broad and new,
To the ideal tendest.

The measur'd faiths of other lands, the grandeurs
    of the past,
Are not for thee, but grandeurs of thine own,
Deific faiths and amplitudes, absorbing, compre-
    hending all,
All eligible to all.

All, all for immortality,
Love like the light silently wrapping all,
Nature's amelioration blessing all,
The blossoms, fruits of ages, orchards divine and
    certain,
Forms, objects, growths, humanities, to spiritual
    images ripening.

Give me O God to sing that thought,
Give me, give him or her I love this quenchless
    faith,
In Thy ensemble, whatever else withheld withhold
    not from us,
Belief in plan of Thee enclosed in Time and Space,
Health, peace, salvation universal.

Is it a dream ?
Nay but the lack of it the dream,
And failing it life's lore and wealth a dream,
And all the world a dream.

## VIII

BETTER days came in 1876. English friends subscribed generously for the Centennial edition of his works ; and in the early summer he was able to commence those happy health-restoring sojourns at Timber Creek recorded in "Specimen Days." This diary reveals Whitman at his mellowest, most spontaneous and most human ; as, for example, in such a brief passage as this :

Sunday, Aug. 27 [1877].—Another day quite free from mark'd prostration and pain. It seems indeed as if peace and nutriment from heaven subtly filter into me as I slowly hobble down these country lanes and across fields, in the good air—as I sit here in solitude with Nature—open, voiceless, mystic, far-removed, yet palpable, eloquent Nature. I merge myself in the scene, in the perfect day. Hovering over the clear brook-water, I am sooth'd by its soft gurgle in one place, and the hoarser murmurs of its three-foot fall in another. Come, ye disconsolate, in whom any latent eligibility is left—come, get the sure virtues of creek-shore, and wood and field. Two months [July and August 1877] have I absorb'd them, and they begin to make a new man of me. Every day, seclusion—every day at least two or three hours of freedom, bathing, no talk, no bonds, no dress, no books, no *manners*.

The pages shine with a quiet, wistful humour. He hunts for a suitable name for his book of jottings; and is attracted by "Cedar-plums," because, for one thing, they quieted a Camden neighbour who was out of her wits. "Whether there is any connexion between those bunches and being out of one's wits, I cannot say, but I myself entertain a weakness for them"; and so forth, garrulously, revealingly, often even profoundly so. It was of this time that Mr. Burroughs, after speaking of that attractive quality that made one "love him and want always to be with him," wrote: "If Whitman was grand in his physical and perfect health, I think him far more so now, cheerfully mastering paralysis, penury, and old age."

This autumn too (September 16, 1877) he could write to Peter Doyle at Washington in his affectionately colloquial manner: "Pete, if you was to see me to-day you would almost think you saw your old Walt of six years ago—I am all fat and red and tanned—have been down in the country most of the summer, returned the past week—feel real comfortable for me—only I am still paralyzed left side, and have pretty bad stomach troubles still at times—but thankful to God to be as well and jolly as I am."[1]

New friends had begun to gather about him, and to visit him from afar; among them Dr. Bucke, his future biographer and dear friend, and from England Edward Carpenter, whose

[1] "Calamus," p. 169.

"Days with Walt Whitman" gives perhaps the most satisfying of all contemporary portraits of the poet. Mrs. Gilchrist, too, came with her children to spend several years near him in Philadelphia. With returning vigour, he was able once again to visit his old haunts. He gave his Lincoln lecture in New York in 1879; and then went off on a long Western jaunt to the Rocky Mountains, among whose granite peaks and fantastically sculptured cañons he found the landscape answering to his poems. He also renewed his acquaintance with the Mississippi, remaining for several months at St. Louis with his brother Jefferson, companion, thirty years before, of his voyages on its waters. Part of the following summer he spent with Dr. Bucke in Ontario, and upon the St. Lawrence. In 1881 he delivered his Lincoln lecture in Boston; returning again to that city, after a visit to his birthplace at West Hills, in order to superintend the publication of a new edition of "Leaves of Grass." During this stay he sauntered daily under the famous elms on the common, where twenty years before he had so earnestly discussed the last Boston edition with Emerson. He frequented the waterside, and visited friends old and new, going out to Concord to see Emerson, now greatly aged. A few years later he wrote to a mutual friend: "I think I know R. W. E. better than anybody else knows him—and love him in proportion."

The fate of this Boston edition was hardly more fortunate than that of its predecessor.

Submitting to the threats of the Society for the Suppression of Vice, and of the Boston District Attorney, the publishers withdrew it after some two thousand copies had been sold. The affair, coupled with a second defence by O'Connor, in the "Tribune," caused some sensation; and when Whitman took over the book and issued it afresh from Philadelphia the edition was sold out in a single day. This success encouraged him to buy the little house in Mickle Street, Camden, where he spent the rest of his days. It was an improvident venture, and his friends had soon to come to his assistance. First they presented him with a horse and light American wagon, which he delighted to drive at a furious pace along the country roads. Then, against his judgment, they sought (unsuccessfully) to secure him a pension in recognition of his hospital work and consequent illness. Others subscribed through newspaper funds, or sent him personal thank-offerings. Others, again, bought tickets for his Lincoln lectures, for the oration his friend Ingersoll gave for his benefit, or for his birthday dinners. An improvident venture it may have been, but the gifts were most gladly given, and the old fellow needed some place of his own in which to receive pilgrims, some thoroughly untidy workshop and lair wherein he might muse or carouse after his own fashion.

Early in the summer of 1888, shortly after celebrating his sixty-ninth birthday, he sat for an hour one evening in his trap, gazing into the broad glowing flood of the Delaware and the sunset-sky above it. The night brought a further and more serious paralytic seizure. But he pulled through; and with the help of Horace Traubel, henceforward his daily visitor, he was able to resume work on "November Boughs," a medley of prose and poems, now included in his "Complete Prose" and "Leaves of Grass" respectively, especially notable for its description of the conception and writing of the latter in "A Backward Glance o'er Travel'd Roads." Whitman cheerfully took up again the fragment of life still left him, but a nurse and wheel-chair now replaced the horse and wagon. The long winter days indoors weighed heavily on him; but in the summer he could once more cross the ferry in his chair, keenly relishing again all the evidences of progress about him.

His life during these later years, from 1886 to 1892, has often been described, and in its outward limitation lends itself more readily than any other period to description. The materials are fewer and less difficult to handle. The wild hawk was tethered. What a gulf seems to divide these Camden days from those of New York before the war, of the vigils in the Washington wards and the long midnight rambles!

The materials are simpler, the wild hawk tethered. But not tamed, as any one may see who turns the pages of Traubel's too ample diurnal record of the old man's moods and sayings. They are all mere *obiter dicta,* yet any score of those pages conveys a not inadequate suggestion of Whitman's quality ; of the secondary elements at least of that curiously personal individuality which makes almost every word written about him by his intimates vital and provocative. As a matter of fact, we are no more concerned about his opinions of men and events than we are about Samuel Johnson's. In either case it is the speaker who holds us, in however different a fashion.

Toward the end of 1891 he wrote a final poem of greeting to Columbus for his discovering thought, and then sank into the last and most painful stage of his illness. His friends thought he must leave them before Christmas, but in spite of terrible sufferings and a complication of serious ailments he lived on till the next Lady Day. Then at last the too tightly clinging body relaxed its hold ; the pain of its holding ceased ; the wonderful irradiating smile returned. Traubel sat by him. The rain fell softly—the rain that gives back life to its own origin. Night came. The great child-like spirit, wise with fullness of days, went forth willingly into the kindly dark.

How welcome must death have been to him who had ever dwelt lovingly upon it ! He had but lately written :

. . . I myself for long, O Death, have breath'd
 my every breath
Amid the nearness and the silent thought of thee.
And out of these and thee
I make a scene, a song (not fear of thee,

Nor gloom's ravines, nor bleak, nor dark—for I do not fear thee,
Nor celebrate the struggle, or contortion, or hard-tied knot)
Of the broad blessed light and perfect air, with meadows, rippling tides, and trees and flowers and grass,
And the low hum of living breeze—and in the midst God's beautiful eternal right hand,
Thee, holiest minister of Heaven—thee, envoy, usherer, guide at last of all,
Rich, florid loosener of the stricture-knot call'd life,
Sweet, peaceful, welcome Death.

His body was laid in the tomb he had had built after one of Blake's noble designs, in the outlying Harleigh Cemetery. It was the beginning of spring. A blue-bird sang on a beech-spray overhead.

### JOY, SHIPMATE, JOY !

Joy, shipmate, joy !
(Pleas'd to my soul at death I cry,)
Our life is closed, our life begins,
The long, long anchorage we leave,
The ship is clear at last, she leaps !
She swiftly courses from the shore,
Joy, shipmate, joy.

## IX

WITH supreme concentration of will, the poet gives himself up wholly to his inspiration. He abandons himself to it, knowing it to be divine. But also he himself wills it. How he can do so, seeing that it is necessarily beyond his knowledge, is the poet's secret.

Like every creative act, it is a work of faith. And as such it transforms his will into a truly creative power, capable of sowing, through the agency of a printed book, new life in the soul of his readers as it awakens their imagination.

It is essentially the creative power, rather than any magical charm, that distinguishes the major poet. In such a one as Whitman it fearlessly commands the attention of posterity. This power to command attention—to compel, as it were, the assimilation of his poems by future generations—comes to be regarded as a spell even when it cannot claim the title of charm. Its effect depends primarily upon a prepotency of spirit, only secondarily upon exquisite craftsmanship.

My last word about Whitman and his poetry is that after making every just deduction from its bulk, and ridding it of whatever is not qualified to stand the test of his own standards, there remains a body of the pure treasure; that this residue is endowed with an original vitality which seems unlikely soon to lose its virtue or become commonplace and ineffective; and that this vitality, this inspirational force, when it is at its height, urges its readers in the direction wherein I believe that human evolution must proceed. The rhythms of Whitman's poetry are charged with freedom and instinct with faith.

# BIBLIOGRAPHY

The first view of a large and difficult subject offered in this little book is necessarily partial and incomplete. Much that is essential to a final view is here omitted. The reader of these pages who feels encouraged by them to seek further intimacy with Whitman must turn to his works, now readily accessible, and to the fuller studies provided by his friends.

The copyright editions of " Leaves of Grass " and Whitman's " Complete Prose," which have been quoted in this book, are published by Mr. Kennerley, of New York. There is also a ten-volume " Camden " edition of the complete works (which includes the letters—also published separately as " Calamus " and " The Wound-Dresser "—with much other matter). For further information lives and studies by the following writers may be consulted : H. B. Binns, R. M. Bucke, John Burroughs, E. Carpenter, W. Clarke, T. Donaldson, J. Johnston, W. S. Kennedy, Bliss Perry, J. A. Symonds, and the French life by L. Bazalgette ; also Horace Traubel's " With Walt Whitman in Camden " and " In re Walt Whitman."